WITHDRAWN

Person Perception

Person Perception

ALBERT H. HASTORF
Stanford University

DAVID J. SCHNEIDER
Amherst College

JUDITH POLEFKA
Middlebury College

ADDISON-WESLEY PUBLISHING COMPANY
Reading, Massachusetts · Menlo Park, California
London · Amsterdam · Don Mills, Ontario · Sydney

TOPICS IN SOCIAL PSYCHOLOGY

Charles A. Kiesler, University of Kansas, Series Editor

 Printed in the United States of America. Published simultaneously in Canada. Library of Congress Catalog Card No. 74–123213.

ISBN 0-201-02753-4
FGHIJKLMNO-CO-7987654

Foreword

It is becoming increasingly difficult for anyone to be a generalist in social psychology. Not only is the number of articles published zooming, but new researchable areas of interest are multiplying as well. A researcher finds more fascinating topics these days than he used to, but he also finds himself behind in his reading of all but one or two of them. As a result, the quality of the broad introductory book in social psychology has suffered. No one can any longer be an expert in all of social psychology.

As an alternative, we offer the present series, *Topics in Social Psychology*, directed toward the student with no prior background in social psychology. Taken as a whole, the series adequately covers the field of social psychology, but it has the advantage that each short book was written by an expert in the area. The instructor can select some subset of the books to make up his course, the particular subset depending upon his biases and inclinations. In addition, the individual volumes can be useful in several ways: as supplementary reading in, perhaps, a sociology course; to introduce more advanced courses (for example, a graduate seminar in attitude change); or just for peeking at recent developments in social psychology.

This volume tackles the problem of social perception—the factors affecting the way we see others. It includes discussion of age-old concerns, such as when we like others and when we don't. It also presents and critically discusses recent evidence on such questions about the attribution of motivational states to others as: Did the other *intend* to cause harm to a third person? Undergraduates have always found the topic of social perception interesting, and I think this volume is the best writing on these questions I have seen at this level.

Charles A. Kiesler

Preface

We are certain that some sage has commented that writing a book together is the ultimate test of friendship. We are glad to report that we have survived the strain of writing. (We now must face our students and colleagues who may choose to read it.) The field of person perception is somewhat like an oceanographic chart—it contains some small islands of sophistication amid vast seas of ignorance. We have selected a small number of the islands and focused attention on them. Unfortunately, some significant areas have received too little attention, for example, the large amount of recent research on nonverbal communication. Our decision to focus on a few problems forced us to omit others.

Another problem we faced was deciding to what extent we should emphasize examples. Research in person perception was stimulated by the full range of human experience, which has been richly described in novels and essays. We chose to run the risk of pedantry by being spare in our use of examples. It is our conviction that theoretical organization is crucial and that most people are capable of generating examples from their own experience.

A number of people have helped in various ways. Both Barbara Hastorf and Doris Schneider have been patient. Dr. Robert Kleck read the entire manuscript and pleaded for a number of changes; he met with partial success. Dr. Samuel Himmelfarb made perceptive comments on an early draft of Chapter 3. The comments of Marilyn Park and Jennifer G. Nelson guided us toward less esoteric terminology and clearer exposition than we might otherwise have used. The National Science Foundation has provided research support to all three of us at various times, and some of that research is discussed in the volume. Mrs. Judith

Fukuda, Miss Patricia Morrissey, and Mrs. Mary Kuzmeski were of great help in typing the manuscript.

We would like to thank the following copyright holders for giving us permission to use quotations and figures from their publications: The American Psychological Association; The Free Press; Harcourt, Brace and World; *Journal of Genetic Psychology*; The New York Herald Tribune; Prentice-Hall; *The Journal of Experimental Psychology*; and the Yale Press.

Finally, we must express our affection for two other participants in this venture, Hans and Penny. They are superior nonverbal communicators and ardent perceivers of people.

June 1970

A. H. H.
D. J. S.
J. P.

Contents

CHAPTER ONE

The Issues in Person Perception

There is nothing more important to us, with the exception of ourselves, than the world of other people. Other people are easily able to influence our joys and satisfactions and can cause us sadness and pain. Consequently we are all interested in learning about and knowing other people, and we all have very strong convictions about how we ourselves come to know and to understand other people. For the psychologist the problem is one of perception; but given the relatively short history of social psychology, he can offer fewer scientific data regarding our perception of people than regarding our perception of objects. Moreover, the process by which we gain knowledge of others is clearly a very complex one, as are the stimuli themselves. It is not surprising, therefore, that psychologists have concentrated their efforts on exploring less complex phenomena, such as the perception of size, shape, and distance. Social psychologists have begun to explore how we know others, however; and our goal here is to define some working conceptualizations about person perception, to describe some of the research, and to point to some problems which demand exploration.

How do we know the world? That is a question man has asked himself for centuries. In its earliest forms the question was posed in such terms as: How do we come to experience the shapes and sizes of objects? How do we come to experience objects as having different colors or as being at different distances? The assumption was made that our contact with the world is direct. The focus of the search was on defining the nature of the physical stimuli which directly cause such experiences. In time the search was extended to the more subtle exploration of the role played by the perceiver himself in determining his experiences. In addition to his sensory nervous system, his past experience and motivational state were seen to have an impact on now these stimuli are processed. Contemporary research in perception emphasizes the joint contributions of the physical stimulus and of the individual to his knowledge of the world. Although our concern here will be primarily with understanding our perception of other people, we shall root our analysis in the general conception of the perceptual process that psychologists have derived from their explorations of the perceptions of size, shape, and other aspects of their object environment.

Before considering the perceptual process itself, we should like to pause for a moment to point out some ways in which experiences can differ. This step is important because we all use the words "perception" and "experience" to refer to several kinds of events. Any distinctions we make have a certain arbitrary quality, but it seems pertinent to acknowledge that the word "experience" really covers a wide spectrum of events. Our experiences range from vague, unanalyzed feelings or impressions to highly abstract verbal concepts about the world.

We think it is useful to distinguish three classes of experience. The first may be called *raw feelings*. Such feelings are somewhat vague and are not verbally labeled. We all have had the experience (which we usually label with the word "feeling") that something is missing or that something is wrong. We have also had the feeling of familiarity or strangeness. These feelings are very real even though we cannot label them exactly. It is interesting to note that when such feelings are particularly salient, we seem compelled to try to make them clearer by applying a label or pointing to a cause.

Accomplishing this act brings us to a second class, which we may call *verbally described experience*. This is the class of experience of everyday life—the class to which we are normally referring when we use the word "experience." We attach verbal labels to events, objects, and qualities of objects. We categorize events and objects by the use of linguistic labels. In essence, this large class of experience is one we can talk about. Within this class the experiences vary considerably as a function of our labeling activity: think of the difference between the experiences we label as a white ball, a grove of trees, and aggressive behavior. They are all direct experiences, but they differ in their complexity and level of abstractness. The nature of the experience is inextricably bound up with the categorizing process, which is determined by our language system.

The third class of experience, even more abstract, is also determined by our language system. Finding a label for this class of experience is not easy; perhaps the best approximation is "*scientific*" *experience*. We now go beyond the simple perception of objects or events and create categories that group objects or events together. Examples of such abstract experiences are social status, loyalty, and justice. These categories or variables even feel more abstract to us in that it is difficult to point to referents in the external world. Some of the categories do not seem intuitively obvious to us; our awareness of linguistic categorizing is quite salient. In fact, the question has been raised whether to call them experiences or ways of thinking about experiences.

We have made these distinctions because an understanding of the perception of people requires that we keep in mind the three different classes of experience and the importance of language as a determinant of experience. For example, the procedures by which we try to understand our experiences of raw feelings are very different from the ones we use to understand experiences we can describe. Also if we are interested in an individual's raw feelings and we ask him to give them verbal labels and rate them quantitatively, we are moving unwittingly from the first to the second class of experience. When we say that a person rather than his behavior is aggressive, we have moved from the second to the third class of experience.

THE PERCEPTUAL PROCESS

Both philosophers and psychologists have long been intrigued with the nature of the human perceptual process. One explanation for their interest is that man is naturally curious about his contact with the outside world and wonders how his experiences are caused and to what degree they reflect the world accurately. Beyond general curiosity, the reason for the interest stems from an apparent paradox, the basis of which lies in the difference between the nature of our experiences and our knowledge of how those experiences are caused.

Anyone who takes the trouble to think about and to describe his own experiences usually finds himself overwhelmed with both their immediacy and their structure. One's experience of the world is dominated by objects which stand out in space and which have such attributes as shape, color, and size. The immediacy of such experiences becomes obvious if one closes his eyes, turns his head in a new direction, and then opens his eyes again. A structured world of objects is immediately present in awareness, without delay and without any consciousness of interpretative or inferential activity. The world appears to be given to us in experience. Yet a causal analysis of these events indicates a very different state of affairs.

You have opened your eyes and you experience a blue vase about six inches high situated on a table. The vase appears to be at a certain distance, and its shape and color are equally clear. Let us remind ourselves of the causal events that are involved. Light waves of a certain wavelength are reflected off the vase. Some of them impinge on the retina of your eye, and if enough retinal cells are irritated, some visual nerves will fire and a series of electrical impulses will be carried through the sensory apparatus, including the subcortical centers, and will finally arrive at the cortex. This description paints a picture of a very indirect contact with the world: light waves to retinal events to sensory nerve events to subcortical events and finally to cortical events, from which visual experiences result. What is especially important is that this causal description reveals a very different picture than does our naive description of experience. (This causal description led a famous German physiologist to remark that "we are aware of our nerves, not of objects.") Thus we have a conflict between our everyday-life experiences of objects together with their properties and an analysis of how these experiences come to exist. How *does* the human being create a coherent perceptual world out of chaotic physical impingements?

Our world of experience has structure. Let us begin with this fact of experience and explore how the structure may be achieved. First of all, we know that our experiences are ultimately dependent on our sensory apparatus, which for visual experiences would include both the retina of the eye and the sensory neurons connecting the retina to the visual areas of the cortex. This apparatus plays, in a manner of speaking, the role of translator. Light waves impinge on the eyes and we experience color. Sound waves impinge on the ear and we experience pitch. Without the sensory apparatus we would have no contact with the external world. There remains, however, the question of the nature of this translation.

A number of philosophers and psychologists have conceived of the translation process as an essentially passive one, completely determined by the physical properties of the stimulus and by the structure of the receptors and sensory nervous system. They conceive of our sensory apparatus as working somewhat like a high-speed translation device. Physical impingements are looked up and the proper experiential attribute is read out. This conception has led to arguments as to how much of this dictionary is present at birth and how much is the product of our learning history. One reason for the popularity of the passive recording view of perception is the immediacy and "givenness" of our experience. Our experiences are immediate and they feel direct. These feelings led to the belief that the translation process must be automatic and built in.

The primary argument against that position stems from the fact that our experience of the world is highly selective. If we passively translated and recorded stimuli, our world would be a jumble of experiences: while you were reading a book, you would also be aware of the pressure of your clothes on your body and of all the sounds around you. Actually, from a myriad of impinging stimuli, we are aware of only certain objects and certain attributes of the objects. Anyone who has asked two different persons to describe the same scene has been struck by the fact that they often describe it very differently; each selects different events and different attributes of the events. Given this phenomenon, we must be more than passive translators. In fact, we must be active processors of information. The world is not merely revealed to us; rather, we play an active role in the creation of our experiences.

Let us take an example from the research of Robert W. Leeper to illustrate our point (Leeper, 1935). The stimulus he used was an ambiguous picture which can be seen as either an old hag or an attractive young woman (Fig. 1.1a). Continued inspection of the picture usually permits an observer to see first one and then the other. Leeper had the original picture redrawn so that one version emphasized the young woman (b) and another emphasized the old hag (c). Subjects who had been exposed to one or the other of these redrawings found themselves "locked in" on that view when the original ambiguous picture was presented. One hundred percent of the subjects who had had prior experience with the version emphasizing the hag saw the hag and only the hag in their first look at the ambiguous picture; ninety-five percent of the subjects who had had prior experience with the version emphasizing the young woman saw only the young woman when first looking at the same ambiguous picture. The subjects had been given a set to process the input stimuli in a certain way, and they created a structure consistent with that set. Although our experiences are both immediate and structured, extremely complex participation by the organism, including the active selection and processing of stimulus impingements, is involved in their creation.

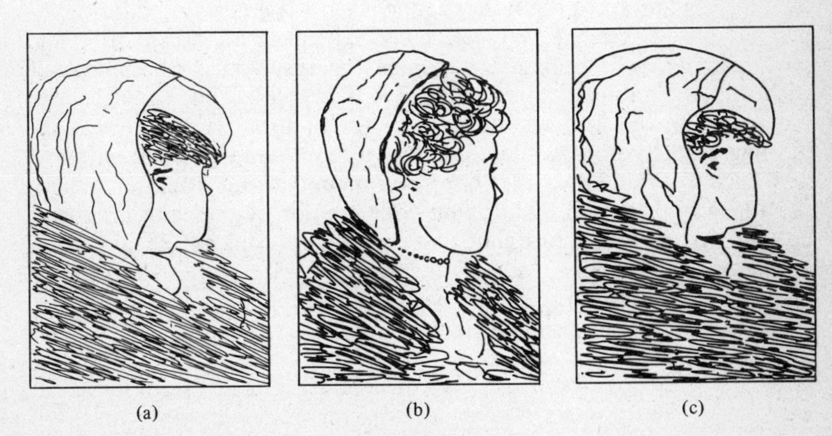

(a) (b) (c)

Figure 1.1

One of the most salient features of the person's participation in structuring his experiential world can be described as a categorizing process. He extracts stimuli from the world and forces them into a set of categories. We have here a powerful example of the effects of linguistic coding on the structuring of experience. The subjects in Leeper's experiment did not see a complex pattern of light and dark nor even "a person" (a possible category); they saw an old hag or a young woman. The categories we use are derived from our past history and are dependent on our language and our cultural background. Some of these categories are markedly ubiquitous and well agreed on by perceivers. Classification of objects according to the attributes of size and shape seems obvious, but some persons may employ different sets of categories. For example, they may perceive in terms of color and softness. Moreover, there are occasions when all of us change categories in perceiving objects. Instead of size and color, we may see things in terms of function: the large blue pen and the small green pencil are suddenly similar when we want only to jot down a telephone number. Whatever the nature of the categories we use, they play an important role in the processing of information.

We have begun with the experiential fact that our perceptions are both structured and organized. This structure is immediate and appears to be given by the world of objects. We have argued that a causal analysis of the situation clearly indicates that structured perceptions are the outcome of the organism's engaging in active processing of information, which includes the translation of physical impingements to nerve impulses and the active selection and categorizing of the inputs.

Our world of experience has stability. When we open our eyes and look at a scene, we are not overwhelmed with constant shifts in the picture as our eyes and our attention wander. There is a certain enduring aspect to our experience. We select certain facets of the situation and stick with them. Check this statement against your own experience with the ambiguous picture in Fig. 1.1. If it was like the experience of most people, the first organization of the picture, whether it was the old hag or the young woman, continued to demand your attention. It was hard to "find" the other one. You made various attempts to shift the focus of attention by blinking your eyes or by concentrating on a certain part of the picture, but those stratagems did not always work. Although stability in a case of this kind may frustrate us to such an extent that it deserves to be given a different and more pejorative label—rigidity—the example demonstrates that we do *not* experience a world of chaotic instability.

The most obvious example of the maintenance of stability in our experience has been termed *the constancies* in perception. Constancy phenomena have been most carefully described in regard to the perception of size, color, shape, and brightness. Let us consider an example. You are sitting in a chair in your living room. Another person walks into the room, moves over to a table by the window, picks up a magazine, and then goes across the room to sit down and read it. What are the successive visual-stimulus events impinging on your retina and your successive experiences? Every time the person moves closer to you, the impingement, or *proximal stimulus*, gets larger; in fact, if he moves from 20 feet away to 10 feet away, the height of the image on your eye doubles in size. The opposite occurs as he moves away from you because the size of the retinal image is inversely proportional to the distance of the object from you. Furthermore, when the person moves near the window, more light is available and more light is reflected to the retina. Yet your perception does not fit this description of the stimulus events. While the person is moving about the room, you experience him as remaining relatively constant in size and brightness. In spite of dramatic alterations in the proximal stimulus, you experience a stable world. Given this discrepancy between proximal-stimulus events and experience, the organism must actively process information to produce the stability in his world of experience.

Psychologists are not in total agreement as to how this information-processing takes place, but certain general characteristics of the organism's contribution are apparent. The organism seems to seek *invariance*; that is, he perceives as constant those aspects of the physical world which are most enduring, e.g., size and shape, even though the information he has about them may change radically. The perceived invariance seems to depend on the ability of the organism to combine information from different sources, and to result from the application of equations which define proximal stimulation as a joint function of the distal stimulus (the object) and environmental mediating factors, such as distance and incident illumination. For example, our person moving about the room is always the same height, say six feet. The height of the retinal image, on the other hand, varies, but it is always a constant direct function of his height and an inverse function of his distance from the observer. An invariant function exists:

$$\text{Proximal size} = K \times \frac{\text{Distal size}}{\text{Distance}}.$$

Figure 1.2 illustrates the relationships. Note that K is the distance from the lens to the retina, which is assumed to be constant. The invariant relationship allows the formula to be "solved" by the perceiver; e.g., knowing retinal size and estimating distance, one can arrive at an estimate of the size of the object. By applying this invariant relationship to a particular case, the perceiver can account for variation in proximal size and perceive the object as of a constant size, as he knows from other

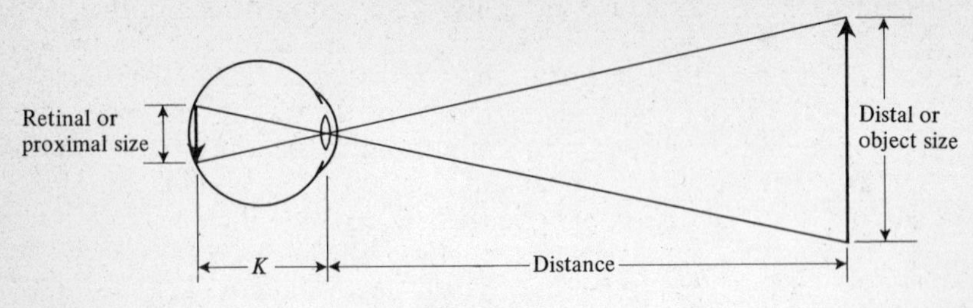

Figure 1.2

experiences it must be. Finding invariance by applying relationships such as the above requires the processing of considerable amounts of information, including the physical size of the object, distance, and illumination; and the information-processing involved in this kind of perceptual act must be quite complicated.

Let us think of the perceptual act as a complex form of problem-solving, the goal of which is to create a stability in which our perceptions bear some relationship to external events. We can then draw an analogy between perceptual problem-solving and scientific problem-solving. Just as the scientist attempts to reduce a complex jumble of events to a small set of variables which serve as a set of determining conditions for a particular event, so we search out the invariant aspects of a situation to produce stable perceptions. The scientist searches for invariance in order to understand and to predict the world; we as perceivers also seek to understand and to predict the world in order that we may behave in it to our advantage. In other words, the perceptual act can be said to generate a prediction that we can use as a basis for action. The goal in both cases is predictability of the environment, and the means to the goal is the specification of causal relationships.

Our world of experience is meaningful. The connotation of "meaningful" here is that structured and stable events are not isolated from one another but appear to be related in some orderly fashion over time. Both structure and stability are probably necessary for meaning to exist. It is so common for the world of experience to make sense to us that the most powerful way to point out the importance of the phenomenon is to suggest trying to conceive of a world that does not make sense. Events would follow each other with no apparent causal relationships. Almost every event would entail surprise. Nothing would seem familiar. The general experience would be one of chaos. Such a state of affairs is so alien to our everyday-life experience that it is extremely difficult to imagine. Our experiences usually *are* meaningful in that they are structured and they are stable; they are related in the sense that they seem familiar, but particularly in the sense that events have implications for one another.

We must look at the organism as an active processor of input stimuli who categorizes stimulus events and relates them to both past and present events. One property of the organism as an information processor is that he possesses a linguistic coding system which possesses a set of implicative relationships. The impinging stimuli provide the raw material; the organism, with the aid of language, produces the meaning. The organism exists in time: he has a past and he anticipates the future. Past experience, language, and present motivational state or goals for the future influence our perceptions of the present. Our past learning has a significant influence on perception, but it always operates within a framework of purposive activity. The experience-derived rules we apply are selected by the purposes we are trying to accomplish. The perceptual process is an achievement by the organism, and perception would not exist without active problem-solving on the part of the perceiver. Our perceptions do have meaning, they do make sense; and meaning and sense derive from both our own past experiences and our present purposes. Without the presence of meaning and sense as active, organizing agents, perception, as we know it, would not exist.

We could cite innumerable studies demonstrating the influence on perception of either the individual's past learning or his present motivational state. Leeper's experiment on the young woman–old hag picture is an example of the former. An experiment by Schafer and Murphy (1943) provides an example of the effects of motivational state on perception. They presented subjects with a simple ambiguous drawing (Fig. 1.3) and gave them a small monetary reward when they indicated that they saw one of the profiles but took money away when they indicated that they saw the other. The results indicated that over time positive consequences associated with a given perception increased the likelihood of that perception. In general, however, we will avoid any precise distinction between a past-experience influence and a motivational influence. The distinction is hard to draw, and attempting to do so could lead us to forget that all behavior and all perception include the influences of both the past experiences and the purposes of the organism.

Historically these two powerful determinants of our perceptions have unfortunately often been termed distorting influences. Perception

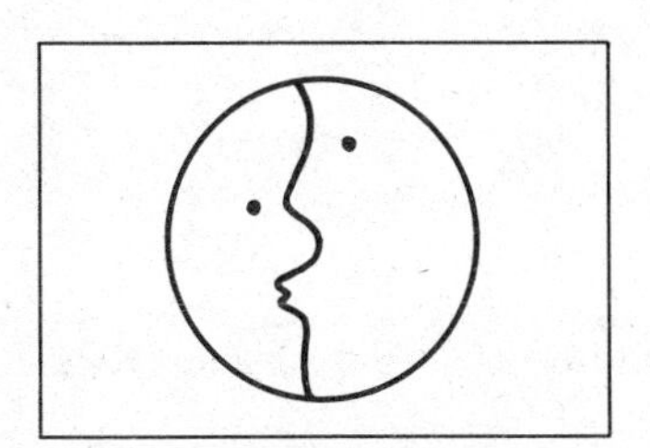

Figure 1.3

was thought to be stimulus-determined unless past experience or motivational state entered the picture and caused us to deviate from "what we ought to see." The notion of the existence of an "objective observer" who sees the world accurately because he has had no past experience or is disinterested is patently false. If such a person did exist, we would have to predict that he would not see a structured, stable, and meaningful world.

In summary, our past experiences and purposes play an absolutely necessary role in providing us with knowledge of the world that has structure, stability, and meaning. Without them, events would not make sense. With them, our perceptions define a predictable world, an orderly stage for us to act on.

THE PERCEPTION OF PEOPLE

Let us now turn our attention more explicitly to the perception of other people. The characteristics of the world of experience in general should hold for our experiences of people, but are there special facets to our experience when we perceive other human beings? Is there not more to our experience of other people than their size, color, and shape? The answer is certainly "Yes."

As an aid in our discussion of person perception, let us consider an example of one person describing another. In *Eminent Victorians*, Lytton Strachey describes Dr. Thomas Arnold, Headmaster of Rugby School:

> Such was the man who, at the age of thirty-three, became headmaster of Rugby. His outward appearance was the index of his inward character: everything about him denoted energy, earnestness, and the best intentions. His legs, perhaps, were shorter than they should have been; but the sturdy athletic frame, especially when it was swathed (as it usually was) in the flowing robes of a Doctor of Divinity, was full of an imposing vigour; and his head, set decisively upon the collar, stock, and bands of ecclesiastical tradition, clearly belonged to a person of eminence. The thick, dark clusters of his hair, his bushy eyebrows and curling whiskers, his straight nose and bulky chin, his firm and upward-curving lower lip—all these revealed a temperament of ardour and determination. His eyes were bright and large; they were also obviously honest. And yet—why was it?—Was it in the lines of the mouth or the frown on the forehead?—it was hard to say, but it was unmistakable—there was a slightly puzzled look upon the face of Dr. Arnold.*

*Lytton Strachey, *Eminent Victorians* (New York: Modern Library, 1933), pp. 193–194. Quoted by permission of Harcourt, Brace and World; Mrs. A. S. Strachey; and Chatto and Windus.

First of all, this description is a special example of person perception in that it is more organized than many of our experiences in everyday-life, partly, no doubt, because the author is attempting to communicate explicitly his perceptions to others. The author also goes well beyond just providing us with a description of Dr. Arnold's physical characteristics and behavior. Many of the characteristics listed are the result of inferences by the author, and yet they are cast as if they were just as clear and as given in experience as is the individual's physical height. The leap from describing such characteristics as hair color and eyebrows to inferences about "energy" and "ardour and determination" is made with considerable agility. The author also includes statements about Dr. Arnold's intentions; he appeared, at least to Mr. Strachey, as having "the best intentions." This tendency not only to perceive others as having intentions but also to make a value judgment about the intentions is, as we shall see, often apparent in our perception of others. The description also includes inferences (stated as perceptual facts) about enduring personality characteristics, such as "honesty" and "eminence." Finally, although the author cannot specify the cues, he infers that Dr. Arnold felt puzzled; he perceives the other's feelings. We can use the characteristics of this description to point out some of the special features of our perception of other people and the ways in which the perception of people differs from the perception of objects. As we noted earlier in our discussion of the constancies, the stimuli produced by objects vary as a function of the conditions under which they are perceived. This is also true of people as stimuli. Furthermore, people behave and behavior is a dynamic rather than a static thing; it is ever-changing and must be carved up into units in order that we may define the stimulus. One of the major ways we separate our ongoing behavior into distinct units is by taking into account behavioral effects. The individual does something and we observe its effect. In essence, the first level of coding in person perception consists of grouping together acts and effects to create manageable perceptual units.

Let us now turn our attention to two very crucial facets of our experience of other people. The first is that we perceive them as *causal agents*. They are potential causes of their behavior. They may intend to do certain things, such as attempting to cause certain effects; and because we see them as one source of their actions, we consider them capable of varying their behavior to achieve their intended effects. (This position was formulated by Heider [1944, 1958] and will be considered in a later chapter.) Our perception of others' intentionality leads us next to organize the behavior of other people into intent-act-effect segments which form perceptual units. We infer the intentions of another; but we go further. If we perceive a particular intent on several occasions, we are prone to perceive the other as having an enduring personality characteristic. A person who seems to intend to hurt others much of the time will be quickly labeled as hostile. Our verbal label now becomes more abstract because we are categorizing the person according to a characteristic which endures over time.

Second, we perceive other people as similar to ourselves. Hence we are pushed to infer that they possess attributes which, unlike size and behavior, we cannot observe directly but which we are aware of in ourselves. In particular, we perceive others to possess emotional states; we see them as feeling angry, happy, or sad. On some occasions these experiences are of fleeting or temporary states; however, if we perceive them often enough in a person, we code or label that person as having that state as an enduring characteristic; e.g., chronically sad people are depressed.

We can now take a brief look at how our three attributes of experience (structure, stability, and meaning) relate to the perception of people.

Our experiences of other people are structured. Just as we create structure in the inanimate world by categorizing stimuli into objects and their attributes, so we create order in the world of people by categorizing them and their behavior. The number of ways that we can categorize people is overwhelmingly large; we can go well beyond any of the possible schemata for inanimate objects. The dictionary, for example, contains thousands of trait names describing ways in which we can perceive people as different. Often we use categories which have been functional in the past. The football coach will employ very different categories for perceiving members of the freshman class than will the Dean of Students or a professor of physics. You may remember that the description of Dr. Arnold by Mr. Strachey was heavily couched in "good Victorian" words like "vigour," "eminence," and "determination" rather than those we might be more likely to use today, such as "warm," "happy," or even (given Dr. Arnold's position) "intellectual."

Dornbush *et al.* (1965) demonstrated that our past experiences and our present motives affect the categories we use when they explored the categorizing activities of ten- and eleven-year-old children at a summer camp. Children who had lived together in the same tent for two or three weeks were requested in an interview situation to describe their tent mates. The interviewer carefully avoided stipulating any categories; he asked the children to "tell me about ———." The interviews were then coded in order to classify the categories the children had employed in describing one another. An example of a category is "neatness." A statement was classified in this category if it described the other person as being either neat or sloppy. The authors were primarily interested in category usage, not in where the person was placed within the category.

Especially pertinent to our thesis is a comparison of the categorization employed by a common perceiver of different stimuli with the categorization by two different perceivers of a common-stimulus person. The category overlap was greatest when one perceiver described two different children (57%); the overlap for two different perceivers describing the same stimulus person was smaller (45%) and not very different from the overlap obtained (38%) when the descriptions of two different perceivers, each describing a different person, were compared. The last figure was interpreted as the amount of overlap created by a common culture. These data imply that the perceiver plays a dominant role in selecting the characteristics of other people to be observed (and described). He does not passively record the attributes of the other person, but selects and organizes his perceptions in terms of categories which are particularly useful to him.

However, we should be very cautious in designating an individual described by two perceivers as "a common-stimulus person." It is highly likely that when one person interacts with different people on different occasions, he is really not the same stimulus person. His behavior will vary as a function of the situation, which includes the nature of the other participants. This fact is an example of the complexity of both social interaction and person perception. How you categorize and perceive me will influence how you behave toward me, and your behavior, in turn, will influence how I behave. Our point, for the moment, is to stress the role the selecting and categorizing activities of the perceiver play in *creating* his perceptions of the other and in producing structure in his world of other people.

Our experiences of other people have stability. The behaviors engaged in by another person vary widely over even brief periods of time; thus the interpersonal acts of another provide as continually varying a stimulus as the size of his body provides the retina when he walks across a room. Were we to perceive as discrete all the acts of another person, our experiential world would be as rapidly changing and unstable as our experience of his size if that were dependent merely on the size of the retinal image. The stability in our experience of other people seems to be produced by processes analogous to those involved in the constancies in perception. We search to perceive the invariant properties of other people.

In perceiving attributes of another person, we focus not on his behavior, which is ever-changing, but on more invariant characteristics, namely, his intents and purposes. Since these invariant properties cannot be perceived directly, our search for invariance is centered on discovering functional relationships between behavior-effect sequences, which are observable, and intentions, which are not. For example, suppose that another person shoves you in the hall, verbally abuses you in a class, and criticizes your friends in private. The behaviors and the contexts in which they are expressed differ, but the same end is achieved: the other person hurts you. Yet the effect is an invariant function of the behavior and the context, just as proximal size is an invariant function of object size and distance. In the attribution to him of the intent to hurt you, an invariance will have been achieved. Whenever we can assume that the person had the ability to produce the behaviors and hence the effects, when we can assume that he was the cause of what occurred, we tend to attribute to him the intent of producing the effect. This attribution of intent provides us with knowledge which will make our future interactions with the person more predictable.

Should we observe the same person behaving in a similar manner toward others, we go further and attribute to him the dispositional property of desiring to hurt other people; we consider him hostile or aggressive. This attribution of a dispositional property to another results again from the search for invariance. If we can classify a person according to certain traits or concepts, we can increase the predictability of our interpersonal world. An aggressive person will act to hurt not only us but others as well. We can predict his behavior in a wide variety of situations. It is also possible that such inferences about enduring dispositions will lead us into dramatic misperceptions. It is very disruptive for us to perceive as failing a person we "know" to be capable and to be trying hard. This is especially true if we have some strong loyalty to or identification with him. That our dispositional inferences can lead us astray was amusingly pointed out by the sports columnist, Red Smith:

> You see, Steve Ellis is the proprietor of Chico Vejar, who is a highly desirable tract of Stamford, Connecticut, welterweight. Steve is also a radio announcer. Ordinarily, there is no conflict between Ellis the Brain and Ellis the Voice because Steve is an uncommonly substantial lump of meat who can support both halves of a split personality and give away weight on each end without missing it.
>
> This time, though, the two Ellises met head-on, with a sickening, rending crash. Steve the Manager sat at ringside in the guise of Steve the Announcer broadcasting a dispassionate, unbiased, objective report of Chico's adventures in the ring. . . .
>
> Clear as mountain water, his words came through, winning big for Chico. Winning? Hell, Steve was slaughtering poor Fiore.
>
> Watching and listening, you could see what a valiant effort the reporter was making to remain cool and detached. At the same time you had an illustration of the old, established truth that when anybody with a preference watches a fight, he sees only what he prefers to see.
>
> That is always so. That is why, after any fight that doesn't end in a

> clean knockout, there always are at least a few hoots when the decision is announced. A guy from, say, Billy Graham's neighborhood goes to see Billy fight and he watches Graham all the time. He sees all the punches Billy throws, and hardly any of the punches Billy catches. So it was with Steve.
>
> "Fiore feints with a left," he would say, honestly believing that Fiore hadn't caught Chico full on the chops. "Fiore's knees buckle," he said, "and Chico backs away." Steve didn't see the hook that had driven Chico back. . . .*

Our experiences of other persons are meaningful. We see other people as organized entities, and nearly always their behavior makes sense. Nonetheless, the behavior of others does confuse and puzzle us on occasion. It is probably a good guess that if a person is consistently puzzling to us, our inability to make sense of him leads us to avoid further interactions with him. No wonder the behavior of most of the people we "know" makes sense!

What are the processes by which we develop these organized perceptions of others as meaningful entities? First, as already pointed out, we organize their behavior into intent-act-effect units, and that procedure not only enables us to develop some behavioral organization but also permits and even pushes us to develop some hypotheses covering the enduring intents and dispositions or personality traits. Second, meaning derives from the fact that other people are similar to one another and to ourselves. We all share a certain number of important characteristics; we all behave, think, and feel; and some of the structured meanings we experience derive from the assumption that other people are like us. The assumption of similarity—"That's the way I would feel"—can lead to assumed relationships between both behaviors and intents. Even though the process may not be conscious, we often operate as follows: "I engage in behavior *A* and also in behavior *B*;" therefore, "if he engages in behavior *A*, then he must also engage in behavior *B*." The same operation would apply to intents and feelings. This process is one of the sources of what we shall later call *implicit personality theory*; it produces assumptions about relationships between personality traits in other people, so that knowing some things about a person permits us to infer other things. The process does not imply that the inferences are necessarily correct, however.

Finally, meaning derives from familiarity. When we have coded a person's behavior in a similar way a number of times and have made the same inferences about the causes of the behavior, then meaning and the feeling of understanding may result. This is especially true when

---

*Red Smith, *New York Herald Tribune*, December 21, 1951.

we perceive that certain traits are correlated. A behavior is familiar not only in that we have seen it before but also in that it implies other behaviors. Implicit personality theories, the assumed correlations between traits which we carry around in our heads, are generalizations from behavior we may have observed in ourselves and one or two other persons. Once we have acquired these theories, we can then apply them as a general rule. The process is identical to that which produces a phenomenon usually called *group stereotypes*.

One way in which we simplify the complex world of other people is to organize them into groups. We talk of Germans, Jews, and Italians; of college students, policemen; even of little old ladies in tennis shoes; and we attribute certain characteristics to all members of each group. On reflection, we are all perfectly willing to grant that college students come in all different shapes and sizes and with very different orientations toward the world; yet we still find ourselves classifying people into groups and then imputing certain characteristics to the members of the groups. We neglect both situational pressures and disconfirming evidence in our push to categorize a person according to his group membership. Fink and Cantril (1937), using college students as subjects, demonstrated this tendency in a study which was concerned with analyzing certain stereotypes students have of one another. A group of undergraduates at Harvard, Yale, Princeton, and Dartmouth were presented with a list of 50 adjectives, such as athletic, brilliant, conceited, juvenile, sophisticated, and studious. Each student was asked to select the five adjectives which best described a Harvard man, a Yale man, a Princeton man, and a Dartmouth man. The first findings of interest were that students made their selections with very little hesitation and that there seemed to be considerable agreement among them as to the nature of the stereotypes they held concerning students both at other institutions and at their own. For example, when 100 student subjects at Dartmouth were asked to describe a Harvard man, the majority of the 500 adjectives selected came from only 10 to 15 words out of the 50 available. When students described themselves, they chose adjectives that were somewhat more complimentary than those they chose to describe others. For example, in describing themselves, Harvard men were most likely to select the following five adjectives: blasé, intellectual, cultured, sophisticated, and broad-minded. Students at Dartmouth, Princeton, and Yale agreed with parts of the Harvard man's self-stereotype; they too saw him as blasé, sophisticated, and intellectual, but added snobbish and conceited, somewhat less complimentary adjectives, to complete the list. Although the study was conducted some years ago, similar findings would probably be obtained today. The adjectives included in such a study today would be different, and the specific content of the stereotypes might have changed in the intervening years; but the tendency to classify people into groups and to attribute certain personality traits or dispositions to the members of those groups is still present.

Our impressions of another person are also a form of stereotype; we abstract certain aspects of his behavior, orgainze them around certain dispositions, and develop a picture of the person. This process permits the development of meaning in our experience of other persons. It can also restrict our awareness of some of another's behavior. Group and individual stereotypes do create stability and meaning; but they may well do it at the risk of inaccuracy.

SUMMARY

We have now set our task. We have identified certain characteristics of our world of experience, which includes the world of other people. It has structure, it has stability, and it has meaning. Furthermore, we have specified an approach to the perceptual process which assumes that perception is not the passive translation of physical energies into experience but is a process demanding active participation by the perceiver. He selects and categorizes, he interprets and infers to achieve a meaningful world in which he can act. We have also described some special features of our perception of other people. Behavior is one of the main sources of stimulation, and it is both complex and ever-changing. One of the ways we make sense out of the complexity is to make inferences that go beyond the behavioral data. We perceive other people as causal agents, we infer intentions, we infer emotional states, and we go further to infer enduring dispositions or personality traits. The social psychologist is interested in this process because it is one of the most salient outcomes of social interaction and, by the same token, one of the major determinants of the nature of interactions. One of the major variables which influence our behavior vis-à-vis another person is the sort of impression we have formed of him and the dispositions we have attributed to him.

The remaining chapters of this book will focus on three important problems. First, what are the principal determinants of our experiences of another person's emotional states and personality dispositions? What stimuli affect those experiences? What variables seem to promote accuracy in those inferences? Are some people more accurate than others? Second, how do we go about forming an impression of another person? In what ways do we combine various bits of information in order to come up with an organized impression? What kinds of information influence us most? Third, what are the processes by which we attribute enduring states to other people? What sorts of variables influence our attributions? If we see another person as trustworthy, what conditions were necessary for the development of that inference? Are there types of social situations which either promote or hinder the development of such inferences? Finally, throughout our consideration of these questions, we will be concerned with the relationship of person perception to interpersonal behavior because perception both guides behavior and is in turn influenced by behavioral events.

CHAPTER TWO

Accuracy in Person Perception

INTRODUCTION

We perceive persons as unitary entities possessing certain physical and personality characteristics, thoughts, and feelings. The attributes of a person vary in several ways. Physical and personality characteristics are relatively enduring properties of the person; thoughts and feelings are more fleeting. Our ideas about other people also vary according to whether they stem from overt, easily observable characteristics of the person or from inferences on our part. Physical characteristics and strong emotional states are noticeable, intrusive characteristics of persons. Another's thoughts may be expressed, or we may infer them. Perhaps one of the most salient aspects of another is his emotional expression. We typically assume that how a person "looks" reflects some inner emotional or feeling state.

Historically, research regarding the accuracy of our perceptions of the diverse characteristics of others has been divided into two topic areas: the perception of emotions and the perception of personality characteristics. The major difference between the areas has been the focus of the research. The goal of those interested in the perception of emotions was to identify the stimuli which elicit our perception that the other person is experiencing a certain emotion: when we experience the other as being happy, what are the facial features that serve as significant stimuli for such an experience? Does the mouth (a smile) or do the eyes play a role? This approach represented an extension of a traditional concern of students of perception to a new quality of experience. Having specified the aspects of physical stimuli which are correlated with the experiences of color, pitch, and pain, we wished to specify, in like manner, the stimuli which lead to the perception of specific emotions.

On the other hand, psychologists interested in our experiences of more enduring characteristics of others were concerned primarily with identifying differences in accuracy among perceivers and with characterizing the more accurate and less accurate perceivers. Since the issues raised in these two areas are somewhat different, we will make the same distinction. In the section immediately following, we will discuss the accuracy of judgments of overt behavior, principally of emotional expression; and in the next section, we will deal with the accuracy of more indirect inferences about personality traits.

ACCURACY IN JUDGING EMOTIONAL STATES

The assumption implicit in research regarding the accuracy with which we judge the emotional states of others came from Charles Darwin's *The Expression of the Emotions in Man and Animals* (1872). Darwin argued that expressive movements associated with emotions had no functional value per se, but represented remnants (or their derivatives) of movements which had been functional for a certain species. For example, the facial expression of disgust bears a close resemblance to the posture of the face during vomiting; and it is possible to argue that the former expression is derived from the latter. That these expressions are communicative was attributed to their origin as functional movements. In accepting Darwin's position, the experimenters adopted two implicit assumptions. First, they assumed that certain facial features are always associated with certain emotional states; a smile means that a person is truly happy. The implication here is that certain overt cues indicate a particular emotion. Second, the experimenters assumed that all perceivers know which cues are associated with which emotions. If a person expresses cues to sadness, all perceivers will perceive sadness. Questions about individual differences in either expression or perception were not raised. The problem was often referred to as that of the *recognition* of emotional states. Thus Darwin's argument convinced psychologists that an individual has the potential to perceive the emotional state of another accurately.

Darwin's book also had an effect on early psychological studies concerned with the identification of emotion; in essence, his studies provided a model for later researchers. He had presented several photographs, each showing a different facial expression of a man, to a number of judges and had asked what feelings the man was experiencing. Some photographs were "correctly" labeled by the majority of his judges, but others produced a variety of identifications. Because of the discrepancies among the stimuli, the intended emotions, and the responses of the judges (who were ignorant of the intention), Darwin felt that suggestion—set and instructions—must play a role in the identification of emotions. It is also true that Darwin was strongly committed to the hypothesis that there are biologically determined links connecting stimulus, experienced emotion, and emotional expression; it is therefore not surprising that he localized the inconsistencies in his data to the link between emotional expression and the perception of it. We see here the first acknowledgement that the process leading to the perception of emotions might be more complicated than was originally assumed.

One study based to a large part on Darwin's assumptions and employing a similar method was conducted by Feleky (1914), who had a series of photographs taken of herself while she tried to portray emotions such as "agreeable surprise," "hate," and "pity." She then presented some of the photographs to judges, who were asked either to select a name or set of names from a long list of emotions or to produce their own labels to describe the emotion a particular pose suggested to them. The extent to which the judges agreed on the emotion portrayed varied for different poses. For example, almost all judgments of the "surprise" pose could be coded into one of 17 categories, and 52% were accurate in the sense that the label chosen was "surprise." On the other hand, 29 different words were chosen to label the "hate" pose and only 8% of the observers "correctly" labeled the emotion as hatred. The lack of substantial agreement between the emotion intended and that perceived in this study and Darwin's suggests either that expressions of emotion are not habitual or biologically characteristic of a species, or that some judges lack the skills to identify the emotions correctly.

R. S. Woodworth (1938) thought Feleky had underestimated the extent of agreement and accuracy in the judgments of her subjects, and he reanalyzed some of her data. First, he combined all the judgments with labels he considered synonymous and discovered that the percentage of accurate judgments increased; for example, when he combined the judgments of "wonder," "astonishment," and "amazement" with those of "surprise" (the emotion intended), accuracy increased from 52% to 77%. Next, Woodworth attempted to order the poses of the intended emotions in such a way as to describe the magnitude of a judge's error: poses most often confused were placed in adjacent categories. Having ordered the poses in that manner, Woodworth noted that certain emotions were often confused: love, happiness, mirth; fear and suffering; anger and determination. He combined the photographs in those groups and produced a unidimensional, six-category scale in which the categories most often confused were adjacent: love-happiness-mirth; surprise; fear-suffering; anger-determination; disgust; and contempt. Using these broader categories of emotion, Woodworth was able to show that subjects were much more accurate than Feleky had concluded from her more specific categories; the median percentage of correct identification in Woodworth's analysis was 78% (range, 60–93%). Thus Woodworth demonstrated that we can accurately discriminate among broad categories of emotional state, if not among highly specific emotions, and that the extent of our ability to discriminate between any two emotions could be represented by the distance between the emotional categories along a unidimensional scale.

Woodworth's six-category, unidimensional scale was the first attempt to describe and quantify our phenomenology regarding the emotional states of others. A number of years later Schlosberg (1952) pointed out that since judges tend to confuse the photographs in the love-happines-mirth category with those in the contempt category, which is at the opposite end of the scale, it would be better to arrange the categories in a circle and to think of them as varying along two bipolar dimensions, which he labeled pleasant-unpleasant and attention-rejection (Fig. 2.1). Later, on the basis of physiological theories of emotion, Schlosberg (1954) suggested that facial expressions of emotion might also vary along a third dimension, sleep-tension.

In recent years several researchers have concerned themselves with the number of dimensions that would be necessary to describe the discriminable differences in facial expressions of emotions, and with the problem of determining the most appropriate labels for these dimensions. Most studies discover a strong pleasant-unpleasant dimension; this finding is not surprising because a general evaluative, or positive-negative, dimension appears often in psychology, philosophy,

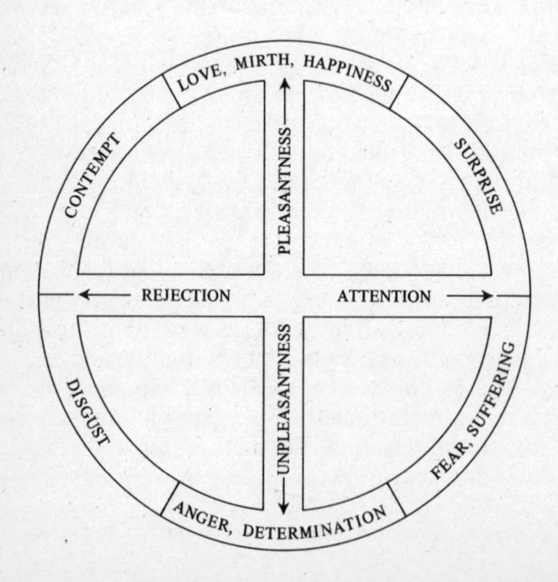

Figure 2.1

and literature, and it is probably a basic dimension of human experience (e.g., see Osgood, Suci, and Tannenbaum, 1957). Researchers seem to agree further that an activity dimension is also quite pronounced. Beyond the evaluative and activity dimensions, however, there is little agreement among investigators on the salient dimensions of emotional expression. Osgood (1966) has recently presented evidence in support of the prominence of both the evaluative and the activity dimension, while at the same time raising the question whether a control dimension should also be added. The disagreements among researchers are due to the nature of the stimuli, to the kinds of ratings requested of the judges, and to the mathematical model used in analyzing the data. A discussion of these issues is beyond the scope of this book, but an excellent presentation of the research findings and methodological problems is contained in Frijda (1969).

It is difficult to make any general statements about our ability to perceive emotions accurately. We have just reviewed evidence which suggests that the degree of accuracy depends on how the judge is to respond, i.e., how finely he must discriminate the emotion and along what dimensions. There is other evidence (see Tagiuri, 1969) to suggest that accuracy depends on such factors as the stimuli employed (e.g., live versus posed) and on the emotions represented.

We should not be surprised to find that evidence to support our belief that we can directly perceive feelings of another is lacking. Attempts to specify the facial-muscle groups involved in the expression of different emotions have yielded inconclusive results. Landis (1924) was unable to demonstrate involvement of particular groups of muscles in all the subjects exposed to any one situation. He took photographs of a number of subjects as they were exposed to a series of stimulus situations, such as observing pictures of nudes, doing mental multiplication, receiving an electric shock, and cutting the head off a live rat. Then he studied the photographs to discover whether any configurations of component facial expression were common to all the photographs taken during a given situation. Some groups of muscles were more likely to be involved under certain conditions, but Landis was unable to identify specific configurations of muscles which predominated in the expressions of all subjects exposed to any specific condition. The reactions of his subjects may have been influenced substantially by the unnatural laboratory situation, however. It may also be true that people exposed to the same situation do not all experience the same emotion; some may feel pleasure and others disgust in viewing a picture of a nude. The results of Landis' experiment are insufficient to disprove Darwin's hypothesis that a specific facial expression accompanies each felt emotion. Nevertheless, the data did induce psychologists to question the concept of biological determination of emotional expression and to move toward a different set of research questions.

It seems that any inherent communicativeness of facial expressions, as was posited by Darwin, has been obscured by the effects of different cultural backgrounds and experiences. Klineberg (1938) gives a series of examples of emotional expressions among the Chinese that differ markedly from our own. Scratching the ears and cheeks is taken as a sign of happiness, whereas rounding and widening of the eyes constitutes a sign of anger. Quite simply, people may express the same emotion differently.

At this point we should remind ourselves that the thesis Darwin offered can be separated into two parts. He was himself more interested in the first hypothesis that there are a number of biologically given (innate) linkages between felt emotion and expressive and gestural signs. Let us call this the emotion-to-expression link. The second aspect was the relation between a person's expressions and our perception of them. Let us term this the expression-to-perception link. Hypotheses about the accurate perception of another's emotion must assume the existence of both links. The work of such investigators as Landis (1924) and Coleman (1949) casts doubt on the viability of the emotion-to-expression link. However, Ekman, Sorenson, and Friesen (1969) have presented data that indicate considerable agreement among observers from the United States, Brazil, and Japan on the identification of the emotions being expressed in certain facial photographs. Although their study has to do with recognition (the expression-to-perception link) of emotions in others, they argue that the high incidence of agreement among observers from diverse cultures implies some validity to the emotion-to-expression link. It is fair to say that the recent work of Ekman and his colleagues has reopened the whole question of the emotion-to-expression link. Prior to its publication, research emphasis had been shifting toward an exploration of the cues utilized by the perceiver in identifying an emotion, with no great concern as to whether those cues were direct reflections of the particular emotion.

Finally, the research we have reviewed relies heavily on identification of emotion from photographs, but in real life we are not limited to simple observation of facial cues. For example, we have available a variety of so-called paralinguistic cues (e.g., voice inflection, rate of speech, etc.) as well as other nonverbal kinesthetic cues (posture, orientation of the body, style of body movement, etc.). There is a developing literature (see Tagiuri, 1969; Davitz, 1964) on the accuracy of inference from such cues, but most of the recent research has concentrated on the determinants of inferences from such nonverbal communications rather than on the accuracy of the inferences themselves.

One example of a significant cue for our perception of the other person is eye contact. Exline and his colleagues (1965) have shown that mutual eye contact seems indicative of positive feelings between people. A recent experiment by Ellsworth and Carlsmith (1968) demonstrates that a high incidence of eye contact may or may not lead to positive affective feelings as a function of the content of the discussion. They varied the frequency with which the interviewer (the experimenter) glanced at the subject's eyes during an interview, as well as the degree to which the content of the interview was pleasant or unpleasant. High incidence of eye contact with pleasant content led to positive feelings, whereas high incidence of eye contact with unpleasant content led to negative feelings; the results were reversed when eye contact was minimal. It is clear that there is much more to the stimulus situation than a static facial expression such as a smile; an eye glance is a dynamic bit of behavior, and its meaning is affected by the content of the discussion. Researchers in the nonverbal-communication area are now demonstrating the large number of postural and gestural cues that can influence our perception of others. As the Ellsworth and Carlsmith study illustrates, such cues do not exist in isolation; if content of the conversation can influence the meaning of an eye glance, then context can influence the meaning of the shrug of a shoulder. The central issue must change from an expansion of the list of cues to a concern with the inference processes by which those cues are added together to arrive at a perception. There must be factors that lead to the emphasizing of one cue or the discounting of another. The next important step, we think, will be more direct explanation of the processes by which cues are combined to form the total impression.

Therefore we find that our attempts to explore the stimuli for the accurate recognition of the other person's emotional state lead us into much more complex problems than had been anticipated. Darwin's original notion that certain expressions directly reflect our inner emotional state may be valid; however, it is now perfectly clear that this hypothesis is extremely difficult to evaluate. Our perceptions of the other person's feelings are heavily influenced by context, the labeling process, cultural rules for the expression of emotion, and a host of other variables. It is not surprising that we have shifted our concern away from accuracy to the exploration of some of the inference processes that structure our experience.

THE ABILITY TO JUDGE PERSONALITY TRAITS ACCURATELY

In addition to perceiving the emotional states of others, we are aware that they also possess enduring characteristics or personality traits which presumably are potent determinants of their behavior. Historically, the accuracy question in this area has been directed not so much toward our ability to assess accurately the personality traits of others as toward the identification of the kinds of perceivers who are particularly sensitive to the enduring characteristics of others. The pertinent studies were designed to determine the relative accuracy with which various judges could infer the personality characteristics of others, and to discover the attributes of good and poor judges of personality. Originally, the existence of a general ability to judge accurately the attributes of others was assumed; later the validity of that assumption was questioned.

In our discussion we will treat the problem historically. We will first describe a few early studies and then show how difficult it is to conclude that any real accuracy of perception has occurred. Our purpose is to impress on you that the early researchers assessed intuitively reasonable questions but encountered real difficulties in trying to answer them.

The motivation of those who conducted the early accuracy studies was very pragmatic: accurate judges may well occupy special positions in various social groups by virtue of their ability—or at least, it might be beneficial if they did. It might be functional for the groups involved if leaders were especially accurate perceivers of their followers, if teachers could make veridical assessments of students, if psychotherapists could see patients as they really are. Thus, on the assumption that some people are more sensitive than others, it would be useful to know the characteristics of those who are. One could then use the information to select potential group leaders, teachers, and psychotherapists.

What would we need to know before we could assert the existence of an ability to perceive accurately the personality characteristics of others? If we look to other types of ability, say intelligence or athletic skill, we find that abilities are stable capacities to perform a fairly wide range of related but dissimilar tasks and that, furthermore, people seem to differ in those capacities. An intelligent person can reason more abstractly, remember more things, and work math problems more effectively than someone less intelligent. Similarly, a good athlete has more endurance, is better coordinated, and can run faster than a poor one. Such capacities are about the same over short and long periods of time; tomorrow a good athlete will probably be better than a poor one in physical tasks, just as he is today.

The more general and stable the ability, the more invariant it will be over time and a wide variety of environmental conditions. In the realm of person perception we can say that a person has the ability to perceive others accurately to the extent that he can accurately assess many different qualities in many different people. If he is good at perceiving only hostility but not friendliness, or if he is accurate in perceiving only very close friends, we will probably not feel justified in saying that he has a *general* ability to perceive others accurately. Thus, in asking whether some people have a general ability to perceive others accurately, we have committed ourselves to looking for individual differences in the ability to perceive many different aspects of many different people over time. Our working conceptualization assumes that perceptual accuracy in one situation is associated with accuracy in another.

The early studies in this area, of which we will examine three, were conducted according to the reasoning outlined above. The researchers were looking for judges who could accurately predict different characteristics and behaviors of various persons; they also wished to describe the characteristics of the good and poor judges. In the first study (Vernon, 1933), 48 male students took tests of intelligence, personality, and artistic tendency; they also made a good many ratings of themselves, of other men they knew well, and of strangers. Subjects rated their friends (who were also subjects in the experiment) on the dimensions on which all were tested; they rated strangers by matching examples of handwriting or artwork with photographs or character sketches of the strangers. Accuracy was determined by comparing a subject's judgments with the test performance of the person judged.

Vernon identified three types of judges: accurate raters of self whose self-ratings agreed with test results and with others' ratings of them; good raters of friends; and good raters of strangers. Accurate self-raters were said to have a good sense of humor, high abstract intelligence, and moderate artistic ability. Good raters of friends, on the other hand, were said to be more artistic, less social (slightly introverted), and less intelligent. Finally, good raters of strangers were intelligent, artistic, and not very social. Vernon's study hence provides little evidence that accuracy in judging others is a general trait.

A second study, which employed a somewhat different methodology, was conducted by Estes (1938). He compiled a number of two-minute motion pictures of 15 subjects who had been instructed to do the following: walk into the corner of the room and remove coat and tie; play a modified game of blackjack; hold a lighted match until it is burned out; build as elaborate a house of playing cards as possible; Indian wrestle. The actors in the film sequences had participated in a long-term study of personality, and many judgments of them had been made by trained clinicians. In general, the ratings of the clinicians provided the criterian for accuracy of judgment. In a series of experiments, Estes presented the motion pictures to various groups of judges, including college students, psychiatric social workers, painters, and psychologists. He asked the judges to rate the stimulus persons on personality dimensions or to select the appropriate personality description for each stimulus person from several possible ones. Estes found that he could differentiate good judges from poor judges; the former were better at judging all dimensions for all stimulus persons. Certain personality dimensions (e.g., inhibition-impulsion; apathy-intensity; ascendance-submission) were easier to judge accurately than were others (note, however, the high probability that behaviors relevant to the judgment of the "easy" dimensions were more likely to appear in the films). Some stimulus persons seemed to be more open than others; they tended to be judged more accurately on all dimensions and by all perceivers. Finally, accuracy was greater when judges were asked to make global judgments, to match personality descriptions with a person who appeared in a film clip, than when they were asked to rate the stimulus person on a series of precise dimensions.

Since the best judges were more accurate than the worst judges across all rating scales and all stimulus persons, Estes attempted to discover the characteristics possessed by the accurate judges. He found, for example, that judges who had strong artistic interests tended to have high accuracy scores. However, he could determine no significant relationships between the judges' accuracy scores and intelligence, neurotic tendency, or other personality characteristics.

The last study we will consider was conducted by Dymond (1949, 1950), who tried to develop a scale to measure empathic ability, or accuracy in judging others. She had students rate fellow members of the small groups into which a college class had been divided. She employed six traits: superior-inferior, friendly-unfriendly, leader-follower, shy–self-assured, sympathetic-unsympathetic, secure-insecure. Each subject was asked (1) to rate himself on each trait; (2) to rate another person on each trait; (3) to predict what rating the other would give himself; and (4) to predict what rating the other would give the subject. Two scores were obtained for each subject: the difference between his prediction of the other's self-rating (3) and the other's actual self-rating (1); the difference between his prediction of the other's rating of the subject (4) and the other's actual rating of the subject (2). Dymond reasoned that since both measurements involved the subject's abilities to "take the role of the other" (Mead, 1934) and predict his responses, both must measure empathic ability; the two scores were then summed to provide a Deviation Score. The greater that score, the less accurate was the subject in making his predictions about the reactions of others. Dymond found individual differences among her subjects on the Deviation Score—in itself a trivial finding since random processes would also generate such differences—but she also found that the differences were related to other personality variables—a finding that is far from trivial. For example, the more empathetic subjects tended to have higher performance IQ's on the Wechsler-Bellevue Adult Intelligence Scale and to give answers on the Rorschach Ink Blots that were interpreted as showing greater personal spontaneity.

Before considering various data from similar accuracy studies, we shall concern ourselves with a number of methodological points which emerge from the Vernon, Estes, and Dymond research. First is the question of what each subject was asked to predict about the other. In all three studies subjects were asked to rate stimulus persons on personality dimensions, but they could have been asked to make judgments about stimulus persons' socioeconomic background, mathematical ability, or impulsiveness. The researchers could also have asked for predictions about stimulus persons' behavior, past or future. In short, there is a range of variables which can serve as rating dimensions in the typical accuracy study, and the Estes study should alert us to the possibility that some kinds of dimensions may encourage accuracy more than others.

A second and related question concerns the criterion for accuracy. If *A* rates *B*'s hostility, we must have some measure of how hostile *B* is before we can determine *A*'s accuracy. Vernon used test scores, Estes used the evaluations of trained clinicians, and Dymond employed the stimulus person's own self-rating. There are other possibilities. For example, if we are interested in how hostile person *B* is, we could use standard personality tests, the ratings of people who know *B* well (peer-rating), or perhaps even *B*'s behavior in a standard or nonstandard situation. These criteria (i.e., clinical ratings, self-ratings, personality tests, peer-ratings, and behavior patterns) have been most frequently employed although there are problems with each. There is no guarantee that therapists' ratings are accurate, and furthermore, since therapists often utilize a set of cues (e.g., response to projective tests) which are not available to the average subject, one could argue that therapists' ratings are different in kind from subjects' ratings and are therefore inappropriate as a criterion. Likewise, *B* may have little insight and make poor self-ratings, or he may have friends who are biased judges of personality. Standard tests and behavior measures also pose problems (Mischel, 1968), and indeed we could probably get only fair agreement that any given criterion for accuracy is an appropriate one.

Third, there were differences among the studies in the kind and quantity of information the subject had about the stimulus person. Estes' subjects viewed short film clips of each stimulus person engaging in various kinds of expressive behavior, whereas Dymond had her subjects interact briefly with each stimulus person. We might argue that "true" accuracy requires interaction, perhaps of relatively long duration. Conversely, it may be that accuracy is at its height with moderate information; too much information may be confusing. There is also the problem that when stimulus persons and judges interact, the different judges may elicit different kinds of behavior from the stimulus person. If one stimulus person behaves quite differently toward two judges as a function of the personalities of the judges, it might be said that the judges do not rate the same stimulus person.

Last is the issue we have already raised of generalizing from such research. Before we can conclude that general empathic or other accuracy abilities are involved, we must sample a variety of stimulus persons and dimensions. Both Estes and Dymond used fewer than 10 stimulus persons and relatively few rating dimensions. Furthermore, because the stimulus persons in both studies came from highly selected samples, unknown bias could have been produced.

Studies dealing with characteristics of particularly good judges of others accumulated throughout the 1940's and early 1950's. In 1955 Taft published a review of well over 50 studies devoted to the correlates of individual differences in accuracy. At about this same time, however, it was becoming clear that there were some serious problems with much of this research. Perhaps the most damaging criticism of it has been concerned with the criteria for accuracy. To use the judgments of trained clinicians is merely to ask how well untrained persons can guess the nature of clinicians' judgments; it may tell us nothing about a judge's ability to infer actual characteristics of the person from limited information. The other popular accuracy criterion is based on differences between predicted and actual scale positions on questionnaires or on proportion of correct judgments. It has been suggested that this measure may reflect things other than the accuracy of the judge, that there might be artifacts in the scoring methods used to select good and poor judges.

Hastorf and Bender (1952) pointed out that part of an individual's empathy score might result from projection or from assuming similarity (Fiedler, 1967). In later research (Bender and Hastorf, 1953) judges were asked to predict the responses of four friends to a series of statements. Four deviation scores were computed: (1) *projection*, the difference between the judge's own response and his prediction (a judge who predicts scores for others similar to his own may be projecting his own characteristics to the other); (2) *similarity*, the difference between the judge's response and his friend's response; (3) *raw empathy*, the difference between the judge's prediction and the other's response; and (4) *refined empathy*, a score derived by subtracting the raw empathy score from the projection score. The authors suggested that the particular difficulty in interpreting these scores was that if the judge and the friend he was judging were actually similar in their responses to the items, the judge could gain accuracy credit on the raw empathy score by simply projecting. Consider, for example, a subject who has a score of 32 on the religious value scale, and assume that he rates person *X*, whose score is 37, and person *Y*, whose score is 45. If our subject is a projector and gives ratings of 31 and 33 for the two subjects (i.e., if he gives ratings close to his own score), he will appear to be more accurate in judging *X* than in judging *Y*. If we generalize from this example, we can begin to see real problems. Now imagine two projectors, *A* (whose score is 32) and *B* (whose score is 21), and further suppose that the mean score for all stimulus persons is 37. *A*'s average prediction, which will be close to his own score of 32, will be more "accurate" than *B*'s average prediction, which will be close to his own score of 21. This seemingly greater accuracy is really an artifact of the circumstance that *A* has a score closer to the average of the stimulus persons than *B*. Bender and Hastorf (1953) suggested that in the future researchers might correct empathy scores for the effects of the bias produced by projection.

Later, Cronbach (1955) presented another criticism of measures of accuracy in person perception. He focused his critique on those studies in which a judge was asked to predict another's response to some scale, and accuracy was measured by taking the gross deviation of judges' predictions from the stimulus person's responses. He argued that the accuracy score was made up of four components, which he labeled elevation, differential elevation, stereotype accuracy, and differential accuracy.

The first of Cronbach's components, *elevation*, refers to the tendency of the judges to use the same part of the rating scales that the stimulus persons use. Assume that *A*, *B*, *C*, and *D* all rate themselves relatively high on traits; e.g., the mean of all their responses might be 7. Judge *X*, who tends to use the lower part of all three scales, might have had a mean for all his predictions of 4, while *Y* and *Z* "correctly" used the higher part of the scale with means of 6 and 8, respectively. It is quite likely that the discrepancies between judge *X*'s predictions and the self-ratings of *A*, *B*, *C*, and *D* will be greater than the discrepancies of either *Y* or *Z* simply because *X* habitually uses a different part of the rating scale than the stimulus persons use. Generally the elevation component is treated as a nuisance, and it can easily be corrected by adding to or subtracting from a judge's predictions; in our example, we could "correct" judge *X*'s score by adding 3 points to all his predictions so that they average 7, just as the stimulus persons' responses do.

Differential elevation is concerned with the judge's ability to order differentially the mean self-ratings of all stimulus persons. Assume that across all traits *A*, *B*, *C*, and *D* have self-rating means of 6.0, 6.5, 7.5, and 8.0, respectively. Can the various judges correctly predict those mean responses if we ensure, by eliminating the elevation statistically, that all judges have mean predictions of 7.0, which is the grand mean for the four stimulus persons? Differential elevation is a measure of the extent to which the judge can rank the average self-ratings of a group of stimulus persons.

Third, we have *stereotype accuracy*, which is similar to differential elevation, but here the unit of analysis is traits rather than stimulus persons. The question is whether some judges produce a more accurate ranking of traits averaged across stimulus persons. Do some judges have a more accurate stereotype in the sense that they correctly perceive that *A*, *B*, *C*, and *D* have "more" of trait *M* than of trait *N*? That is, are these judges aware that some traits are more prevalent in the sample of persons rated than are other traits? Again, we would have to ensure that the judges use the same part of the scale, i.e., that they do not differ in their elevation scores. It should be clear that a particular judge could consistently use the "wrong" part of the scale (high elevation score) and not be able to rank-order stimulus persons correctly (high differential elevation error), yet be quite accurate in that he could correctly rank-order traits for the sample of stimulus persons.

Finally, Cronbach discusses *differential accuracy*, which is the ability to predict differences among stimulus persons for each trait. It amounts to that part of the total discrepancy score for our given judge's ratings which remains after the other components have been subtracted. This score is probably closest to what a sophisticated reader of the research literature in this area would regard as a "true" accuracy score because the various "response bias" components (elevation, differential elevation, and stereotype accuracy) have been eliminated.

In summary, *elevation* concerns a bias of the perceiver to use a different part of the scale from that used by the stimulus persons, *differential elevation* concerns the perceiver's ability to rank-order the stimulus persons' total scores, *stereotype accuracy* is the ability to rank-order traits, and *differential accuracy* is the ability to rank stimulus persons for *each* trait.

The immediate effect of Cronbach's article was to render invalid or uninterpretable most of the previous research in this area, since it was not possible to determine how "accurate" judges achieved their scores in the absence of the raw data on which the published reports are based. Cronbach's critique was not entirely negative, however. For example, it allowed a mathematically sophisticated and differentiated treatment of the projection problem raised by Hastorf and Bender. Projection could affect either the elevation or the stereotype accuracy scores and in that way produce seemingly greater accuracy or inaccuracy when gross deviation scores were used.

Two points should be made clear. The first is that Cronbach did not imply that it was meaningless to ask whether one person had greater ability to perceive others accurately. He did suggest that we should analyze how the more accurate person achieves his accuracy. Is it because he uses the scale correctly (low elevation score) or because he has high differential accuracy?

The second point is that Cronbach merely provided a mathematical foundation for such analysis. Mathematically there are several components to accuracy, but empirically some may be trivial or relatively unimportant. In actual studies if no judge "misused" the rating scale, elevation would contribute little to error. Similarly, differential elevation may have a limited role to play in specific studies because judges do not differ in their ability to rank-order people over all traits rated.

In the period since 1955, fewer studies on accuracy of person perception have been reported. To be able to ask and answer the proper questions in this area requires extreme care in collection and analysis of data. Research does continue, nonetheless, and it has largely concentrated on the extent to which the various components contribute to general accuracy and on the implications of various scoring procedures for the relative contributions.

Crow and Hammond (1957) investigated the accuracy issue, using a wide variety of stimulus persons and criteria. They calculated one form of the differential-accuracy score and found that the correlations among various kinds of ratings did not in general differ significantly from zero, a finding they interpret as suggesting that differential accuracy among judges is not general across rating tasks. They also showed that various stereotypic "response sets" are more stable over time for individual judges than are their differential accuracy scores. These findings strongly suggest that general accuracy of person perception is due more to stable response tendencies than to differential accuracy. Cline and Richards (1960) also investigated this problem, and their analysis indicates that the most powerful component of gross accuracy difference among judges was stereotype accuracy.

One might argue in the light of all the suggested qualifications and restrictions that the accuracy question has lost some of its intuitive charm. Certainly we have learned that the scientific investigation of common sense problems results in reconceptualization and the realization that the initial question was not properly put. Three rather distinct trends seem to have evolved from the original accuracy question, however. All three are similar in that they indicate that investigators have moved beyond the naive accuracy question and are showing more concern with the process involved in making judgments about others.

The first trend, which is closest to the original question, is illustrated by the work of Cline (1964). Accuracy is still the main emphasis, but it is explored with careful attention to the nature of the traits to be rated, the type of information available, and a precise statement about the definition of accuracy. A second trend moves away from the accuracy question and focuses on the interpersonal meaning of some of the sources of "bias." For example, "projection," or assumed similarity, had been considered a source of accuracy error. Fiedler (1958) has explored the characteristics and interpersonal behaviors of individuals who seem prone to assume a high degree of similarity with most members of their group, as compared with those of individuals who appear to make finer discriminations. His research indicates that leaders who assume a lot of similarity with all group members employ a leadership style different from that of leaders who do not (Fiedler, 1964).

The final trend entails an explicit shift to a concern with the underlying processes when we make judgments about others. What is going on when one person forms an impression of another? Events that had been termed errors or distortions of accuracy are now looked at as important underlying processes that must be understood in their own right. For example, one such "error" that judges characteristically make in rating another has been termed the "halo effect" (Thorndike, 1920). It refers to the tendency to generalize a positive impression about a stimulus person to all aspects of him. If a person is perceived as kind and generous, then he "must be" warm and trustworthy. The so-called "logical error" (Newcomb, 1931) is similar. If *A* sees *B* as good at English, then *A* is likely to perceive *B* as good at foreign languages. Since ratings of other people are used extensively in psychological and educational research, not to mention letters of recommendation and job performance, it is understandable that such rating biases have been treated as nuisance at best and pernicious error at worst. On the other hand, if a researcher can overcome such a negative "set" toward these phenomena, he may discover not only that such tendencies are ubiquitous, but that they reflect basic tendencies in the perceptions we have of others. Exploration of such tendencies raises more general questions about the processes of forming impressions of other people. It is to this process of impression formation that we now turn.

CHAPTER THREE

Impression Formation

While studies on the accuracy of person perception should and will continue, most recent research in person perception has focused on how information about another is processed. In this chapter we will consider an important area of research on how we form first impressions of another person, and that in turn will lead to a general discussion of how we infer characteristics of another person based on minimal information about him.

Let us begin by stating some assumptions regarding our experiences or impressions of others. We form an impression of another even on making a very brief observation of him or on hearing someone else describe a few of his characteristics. Our impressions are verbalized in terms of traits such as hostile, friendly, aggressive, helpful. These impressions are immediate; we are unaware of making inferences. They are meaningful and organized; we are aware of a person who possesses a coherent set of traits. We know him, in the sense of being aware of his traits and being prepared to predict other traits or behavioral tendencies which we have not observed. Though unique, this individual shares certain combinations of qualities with other individuals we have known.

By what process are discrete stimuli organized to produce a coherent picture of another human being? What factors contribute to the character of the unique, final impression? In short, how are these impressions formed?

THE ASCH PARADIGM

In 1946 Solomon Asch suggested two general models of impression formation. A simple additive model predicts that the final impression is based on the sum of the impressions of the individual traits possessed by the stimulus person. A variant of the same model suggests that the quality of the final impression also affects the quality of each trait; for example, if the final impression is favorable, each trait will also tend to be seen as favorable. Asch preferred a second model, which states that the traits are immediately organized to form a whole, or Gestalt. Thus each trait affects each of the others, and the final impression is a dynamic one not easily predictable from the individual traits taken separately. The final impression is more than the sum of its parts.

Asch performed a series of experiments to explore the adequacy of these alternative models. His method was simple and direct, and it has served as an example for much later experimental work in this area. He presented subjects with a list of stimulus traits which were said to characterize a particular person, had the subjects write a paragraph describing their impressions of the person, and then had them select from pairs of opposing traits the one which they felt would best characterize the stimulus person. In his first experiment Group *A* heard the stimulus person described as: intelligent-skillful-industrious-*warm*-determined-practical-cautious, while Group *B* heard: intelligent-skillful-industrious-*cold*-determined-practical-cautious. The two lists are identical except for the terms "warm" (*A*) and "cold" (*B*). It is clear from the pattern of response traits chosen that quite different impressions were formed by the two groups (see Table 3.1, columns *A* and *B*). Note that many traits, such as generous, were greatly affected by whether the stimulus person was described as warm or cold. Other traits, such as reliable, were seen as being possessed equally by warm and cold stimulus persons.

Asch's position was that Group *A* and Group *B* formed very different kinds of impressions. Perhaps Group *A* subjects (the "warm group") saw the stimulus person as a talented chap who uses his talents to help others, while Group *B* subjects (the "cold group") saw the stimulus person as talented but egocentric and selfish. Asch was also able to show that a stimulus list including neither warm nor cold elicited less polarized responses than one on which warm or cold was included (Table 3.1 column *E*). For example, while 91% of the subjects saw a warm, industrious, skillful, determined, practical, and cautious stimulus person as *generous*, and 8% saw a cold, industrious, skillful, determined, practical, and cautious person as *generous*, 55% saw an industrious, skillful, intelligent, determined, practical, cautious person as *generous*. Clearly the inclusion of warm or cold has acted to increase the uniformity of trait attribution. Given these data, Asch argued that warm and cold constituted central traits; they seemed to bear a large responsibility for organizing the impression his subjects had formed. Other traits did not serve to organize the impression as effectively and did not create polarization of the inferences drawn about the stimulus

TABLE 3.1[*]

Stimulus list *A*	Stimulus list *B*	Stimulus list *C*	Stimulus list *D*	Stimulus list *E*
intelligent	intelligent	intelligent	intelligent	intelligent
skillful	skillful	skillful	skillful	skillful
industrious	industrious	industrious	industrious	industrious
warm	*cold*	*polite*	*blunt*	
determined	determined	determined	determined	determined
practical	practical	practical	practical	practical
cautious	cautious	cautious	cautious	cautious

Percentages of Subjects indicating that trait is characteristic of person

	A (warm)	*B* (cold)	*C* (polite)	*D* (blunt)	*E* (no key trait)
generous	91	8	56	58	55
wise	65	25	30	50	49
happy	90	34	75	65	71
good-natured	94	17	87	56	69
reliable	94	99	95	100	96
important	88	99	94	96	88

* From Solomon Asch, "Forming impressions of personality," *Jounal of Abnormal and Social Psychology*, 1946, **41**, 258–290.

person. For example, when *polite* or *blunt* was inserted in a position previously occupied by warm or cold, the group exposed to the *polite* stimulus person formed inferences that were not radically different from those made by the group exposed to *blunt* (Table 3.1, columns *C* and *D*).

Asch further argued that whether a given trait was central or peripheral in the formation of an impression depended on its relationships to all other stimulus traits (its context). There are at least three testable derivations from that argument. The first, demonstrated above, is that the effects of varying a pair of stimulus traits will depend on the relationship of that pair to the other stimulus traits: the change of warm to cold in the stimulus list affected the impression more than the change of polite to blunt in the same list. Second, if the centrality of traits is indeed a function of other stimulus traits, then in some stimulus contexts warm-cold would not be central traits. Asch did find some evidence that warm-cold are less central when embedded in the list obedient-weak-shallow-unambitious-vain; subjects' responses indicated that the inclusion of warm or cold had little effect on their impressions.

A final implication of the stimulus-context argument is that the same results could not have been produced by the presentation of warm and cold alone. In one experiment Asch found that impressions formed from the warm-cold traits alone were more uniform than those formed when they were embedded in a context: whereas 55% of the subjects saw as generous an intelligent-skillful-industrious-determined-practical-cautious person, 91% saw him as generous if he was also warm, but 100% saw as generous a person who was simply warm. Asch argued that these results supported his Gestalt approach since the other stimulus traits must have "dampened" the effects of warm and cold.

Asch did several other experiments, all of which yielded data consistent with his view that in many impressions there are central traits or pieces of information about the stimulus person which tend to dominate the impression, around which the other traits seem to be organized for their meaning. Certainly that position is close to some of our own feelings about impression formation, and Asch's article contains a wealth of phenomenological description from his subjects which is consistent with his view. Quite simply, a pretty, vivacious, stupid girl is a different creature than a pretty, vivacious, intelligent one. If nothing else, we expect more silly giggling from the former.

Asch's article led to two important lines of research. The first concerns the relationships among stimulus and response traits, and it asks the question whether specification of such stimulus-response relationships will allow a researcher to predict what subjects will infer from a given list of stimulus traits. That research will be considered in the next section. The second line of research concentrates on the way the stimulus information is combined and processed, the way inconsistencies in the stimulus information are resolved. That approach is focused primarily on the relationships among stimuli, and we will consider it in the section entitled "Processes of Impression Formation."

IMPLICIT PERSONALITY THEORY

Asch's Gestalt Position

Asch believed that the stimulus traits produced a coherent impression which in turn facilitated further inferences about the stimulus person. Keep in mind that he had subjects write a description of the stimulus person, a description he believed approximated the impression. For example, one of Asch's subjects wrote the following description of the intelligent-skillful-industrious-cold-determined-practical-cautious person: "A very ambitious and talented person who would not let anyone or anything stand in the way of achieving his goal. Wants his own way, he is determined not to give in, no matter what happens."* If that subject were then asked to check which traits he thought were characteristic of the person he had described, he would probably check traits like strong, important, reliable; he would avoid checking traits like generous, altruistic, and humorous. For Asch the intervening unpredictable impression was capable of generating a set of inferences. It was then a two-step process: stimulus traits → impression → response inferences.

Trait Implications

There is an alternative possibility. Perhaps we generate inferences about another person directly from the information we have; it may not be necessary to assume that an intervening impression has been formed. Given that we know Mr. *A* is cold, we have little trouble believing him to be also unkind or aggressive. That possibility was suggested by Bruner and Tagiuri in their 1954 review of the literature on person perception. They suggested that in the area of impression formation more attention should be paid to the question of how we generate information about others from partial cues. How is it that a warm person is seen as generous, and a happy-intelligent person is perceived to be honest? Bruner and Tagiuri proposed that such inferences were generated by a naive, *implicit theory of personality*. We all somehow have a sense of which traits are associated with which other traits. In the accuracy studies such general beliefs about the distribution of traits among individuals had been considered a frequent source of a

*Solomon Asch, "Forming impressions of personality," *Journal of Abnormal and Social Psychology*, 1946, **41**, 263.

judge's error in predicting a particular person's characteristics. Bruner and Tagiuri suggested that the processes underlying the apparent errors should be studied.

Bruner and Tagiuri took their argument seriously and published some of the early research on the network of inference processes in impression formation (Bruner, Shapiro, and Tagiuri, 1958). Specifically, they were interested in the inferences subjects would draw from knowing a stimulus person is intelligent, independent, and considerate or inconsiderate. For example, given that intelligent people are seen as clever, efficient, not submissive, etc., and inconsiderate people are thought to be aggressive, boastful, discourteous, irritable, etc., what can we predict about an intelligent, inconsiderate person? Asch had suggested that the responses to the two traits taken together could not be predicted directly from the inferences drawn from them individually. Bruner *et al.* showed that inferences drawn from double traits are predictable from knowledge of the inferences drawn from the individual traits. Intelligent people are seen as moderately aggressive, and inconsiderate people are seen as highly aggressive; an intelligent, inconsiderate person is also perceived as aggressive—not a particularly surprising result. But what if the stimulus traits conflict? Intelligent people are responsible, whereas inconsiderate people are irresponsible. What is an intelligent, inconsiderate person? He is seen as somewhat responsible, and this finding turns out to be predictable on the basis of the strength with which each stimulus trait elicits its inference. In this case intelligence elicits responsibility more strongly than lack of consideration elicits irresponsibility. We should be careful to note that such implicative relationships are not always symmetrical. For example, Warr and Knapper (1968) report that their subjects see cynical as implying precision, but precise does not imply cynicism. At any rate, what Bruner *et al.* had shown is that one can account for some final impressions on the basis of responses to the component traits.

Wishner (1960) also studied the relationships among traits when he attempted to reinterpret the original Asch experiments in terms of leads provided by Bruner, Shapiro, and Tagiuri (1958). Wishner had undergraduate subjects rate their instructors on 53 of the Asch traits, and he simply determined from these data the correlations among all traits. Wishner reasoned that if warm and cold make a difference in the selection of response traits, then the dimension warm-cold must be correlated with the response traits; he was able to show quite convincingly that the correlations of warm-cold with response traits do predict how much those traits are affected by the inclusion of warm or cold in the stimulus list. For example, in the initial Asch experiment the warm stimulus person is seen as more imaginative than the cold one. Wishner found a correlation of 0.48 between ratings of warmth and imaginativeness. On the other hand, warm and cold stimulus persons are seen as equally strong, and Wishner found no correlation ($r = .07$) between the two dimensions.

Wishner's article is often interpreted as being critical of Asch, but actually it has merely put Asch's argument on firmer grounds. Admittedly, Asch did feel that more was involved in his dynamic wholes, the Gestalt impression, than correlations among stimulus traits, but Wishner clearly showed that if we know the relationships among traits, we can predict response traits from stimulus traits. He has also provided us with a genuine definition of a central trait. Whereas Asch could only intuit which would be central traits, Wishner showed that a trait is central to the extent that it correlates highly with the response traits. Furthermore, Wishner showed that the centrality of a trait is more a function of the given response traits than of the other stimulus traits, as Asch had suggested. Remember that Asch believed the stimulus traits formed a Gestalt, and therefore the centrality of a particular stimulus trait would depend on what other stimulus traits were present. Wishner clearly showed that centrality of a stimulus trait depends on which response traits are present. Warm-cold would not be central if the response traits did not correlate with warm-cold (the responses checked would not vary as a function of the presence of warm or cold as a stimulus trait). Further evidence for this analysis comes from data collected by Rosenberg *et al.* (1968).

But the most important feature of Wishner's analysis is that he has provided us with a working model of the implicit personality theory. It is simply a correlation matrix among traits, a matrix we all carry around with us. Each of us has an idea of what traits are closely or not so closely related to other traits.

A Short Excursion into Methodology

Much of the support for the idea of implicit personality theory comes from research using correlations among traits, factor analyses of such correlations, or multidimensional scaling of implicative relationships among traits. It would therefore be appropriate to discuss those methods briefly. A correlation indicates the extent of relationship between a paired set of observations. There are various ways of obtaining such data. For example, we could have two perceivers rate the same set of stimulus persons on the same trait. The obtained correlation would represent the extent to which the two perceivers agreed in their perceptions of the stimulus persons. Or we might ask the same perceiver to rate two stimulus persons on several traits; the resultant correlation would represent the extent to which a given perceiver saw two stimulus persons as alike. The most common technique in this kind of research is to have many perceivers rate the same stimulus person on two traits. It will produce a correlation which reflects the extent to which two traits are seen as related. With some modifications this technique was the one used by Wishner, for example.

However, one need not be restricted to correlational methods in studying trait relationships. One could simply ask subjects how similar two traits are, or one could use the implicative relationship measure favored by Bruner *et al.* (1958), in which subjects are asked directly to give their ideas about which traits imply which other traits. For example, Bruner *et al.* asked subjects to complete such statements as "People who are intelligent (very often are, tend to be, tend not to be, etc.) aggressive, active, etc." The advantage of this method is that perceived relationships are obtained directly, whereas with correlations the relationships are generated through standard statistical procedures. Todd and Rappoport (1964), however, report that correlational and implicative measures yield similar estimates of the perceived relationships among traits.

Either method generates a matrix of trait-by-trait relationships, and with several traits there will be many different relationships to consider. There would be considerable advantage to finding dimensions underlying those relationships. For example, if we found that strong, tall, and aggressive were strongly related traits, we would have little trouble inferring a dimension of masculinity underlying that set of relationships.

Table 3.2

Hypothetical correlations among traits

	Warm	Happy	Sincere	Intelligent	Skillful	Determined
Warm	—	.75	.80	.30	.25	.35
Happy		—	.60	.35	.20	.25
Sincere			—	.30	.20	.10
Intelligent				—	.80	.60
Skillful					—	.70
Determined						—

A hypothetical example involving correlations among six traits is given in Table 3.2. Keeping in mind that correlations vary from −1 to +1, note that the correlations are all positive, reflecting the fact that all the traits included are at least somewhat positively related. Note also that there are two distinct clusters of traits: warm, happy, sincere; and intelligent, skillful, determined. Relationships of traits within the clusters are higher than relationships between clusters. The two clusters might correspond to dimensions of social success and intellectual success, respectively, and indeed the traits were purposively selected to illustrate the social and intellectual dimensions found by Rosenberg *et al.* (1968).

Factor analysis and multidimensional scaling are two widely used techniques for specifying mathematically the dimensions underlying a set of trait relationships. The multidimensional-scaling model has come to be recognized as a powerful device for finding dimensions underlying implicative relationships (e.g., Jackson, Messick, and Solley, 1957; Jackson, 1962; Lay and Jackson, 1969; Rosenberg *et al.*, 1968), and factor analysis is useful in exposing the underlying dimensions of a correlation matrix (e.g., Passini and Norman, 1966). It is worth pointing out that factor analysis and multidimensional scaling yield somewhat different dimensions of trait relationships (Todd and Rappoport, 1964), although it is not clear to what extent this finding constitutes a critical problem.

Inferring implicit theories of personality. Cronbach (1955) was among the first to study implicit theories of personality. He analyzed the correlations of judges' trait-ratings for several stimulus persons and was able to show that different judges were employing different underlying dimensions.

One of the more interesting sets of studies which support the idea of implicit personality theory was done by Norman. In one study (Norman, 1963) he collected and analyzed a large set of peer ratings. A clear and rather stable structure emerged, and the number and kinds of dimensions of judgment were very similar for subjects who had lived together for three years in a fraternity and for those who had less prolonged and intimate contact. Norman felt he had isolated some basic dimensions of personality. Passini and Norman (1966), however, raised the possibility that those results could be reflecting perceptual tendencies of the raters instead of real dimensions of the stimulus persons' personalities. They asked subjects to rate people they didn't know but who were in the same room with them, and the ratings used were highly similar to those made by subjects in the earlier Norman (1963) study. More recently Hakel (1969) has found similar results using the trait implication procedure of Bruner *et al.* (1958). Since the same dimensions of judgment seem to arise, whether the perceivers know the stimulus person or not, it is reasonable to argue that the dimensions of perception are implicit in the perceiver. We have previously argued in Chapter 1 that the perceiver has a large role in organizing his perceptual world, and the Passini and Norman research seems to support that contention. In this connection, you may also remember our Chapter 1 discussion of the children's camp study by Dornbush *et al.* (1965), which showed that more category overlap occurs with a single perceiver describing two stimulus persons than with two perceivers describing a single stimulus person.

In the Norman research the implicit personality theory is a general one, and it reflects the perceptions of a group of perceivers making ratings on a standard set of traits. Norman, then, is primarily interested in how the generalized perceiver organizes his perceptions of others, and his research probably says something about the way our culture socializes people to perceive others. There is no implication from this research that such an implicit theory of personality is used in every situation by every individual for all possible traits. The generalized—one could almost say culturally given—implicit personality theory is an obstraction of many individuals' theories, and this theory may not be used completely by any one perceiver. All we are really suggesting is that while this implicit personality theory is extremely important, we should not be blinded to the possibility that some, maybe many, perceivers have theories which vary somewhat from the general theory.

It would therefore be important to study individual perceivers' implicit personality theories. Koltuv (1962), following a suggestion of Hastorf, Richardson, and Dornbush (1958), had perceivers rate others on traits the perceivers provided for themselves. She had perceivers rate others on various traits so that she could determine the relationships among traits for *each* perceiver. She showed that most perceivers did perceive relationships among traits, which she interpreted as evidence of individual implicit personality theories. She also showed that the relationships were usually stronger when the perceivers were rating people they did not know well and for traits which they considered important rather than unimportant. The former finding may well indicate that implicit theories of personality in the form of assumptions about which traits are related to one another operate most strongly when the perceiver faces an ambiguous person, one he does not know well. On the other hand, when the perceiver is rating people he knows something about, such stereotyped inferences are modified to fit actual characteristics of the other more closely. The finding that important traits are perceived as more closely related than unimportant traits may reflect greater articulation within our implicit personality theories for traits we consider important.

If we believe that perceptions of other people are partially determined by perceiver variables, and that individual perceivers may have somewhat different theories about the way other people "really are," then we may be tempted to say that the perceivers' inferences about another reveal more about that perceiver than about the stimulus person.

Just such a position was taken in an influential book, *The Psychology of Personal Constructs*, published in 1955 by a psychotherapist, George Kelly. He argued that we can tell a great deal about a person by how he categorizes others, or by knowing the constructs he uses to describe his interpersonal world. A *construct* is the way any two things are like each other and different from a third (e.g., *A* and *B* are kind, but *C* is cruel). Constructs, then, are like traits, provided we realize that each trait has an opposite trait paired with it so that the two act as opposite ends of a dimension. People differ in the traits they generally use to describe people, but Kelly warns that just the fact that two people say that a given other is kind does not mean that they perceive him in the same way. Kindness may mean different things to two different people, and Kelly determines whether a discrepancy exists by finding out what the opposite of "kind" is for the two perceivers. Perceiver *A* says *X* and *Y* are kind and *Z* is "cruel," but *B* says that *X* and *Y* are kind and *Z* is "hostile." *A*'s construct is *kind-cruel*; *B*'s is *kind-hostile*. Similarly, one person may use a construct *happy-sad*, whereas another uses *happy-dislikes me*. In practice, constructs are hard to pin down precisely, both because there may be distortion and lack of articulation of one or both ends of the contruct and because our common linguistic heritage specifies certain "acceptable" opposites for traits. It may therefore require considerable clinical perceptiveness and insight to find out that a particular perceiver has a construct happy-angry rather than the more traditional construct happy-sad.

Kelly's suggestions have struck a respondent chord with researchers in this area. His work has emphasized the importance of studying the individual perceiver's implicit personality theory, and studies by Walters and Jackson (1966), Messick and Kogan (1966), Shapiro and Tagiuri (1959), among others, have shown individual differences in implicative relationships among traits.

A recent article by Wiggins *et al.* (1969) can serve as an example of research which explores individual differences in implicit personality theory. Judges were asked to rate the intelligence of a number of hypothetical students who varied systematically along several dimensions (e.g., grades, study habits, mother's education, etc.). Their ratings were analyzed in a way which allowed the researchers to uncover eight groups of judges. The judges differed in the way they made their ratings of intelligence, i.e., the way they utilized the various cues. For example, Group I relied most heavily on high school grades in making their judgments of intelligence, Group II relied most heavily on a test of English effectiveness, Group III on grades, English effectiveness, responsibility (a temperament rating), and study habits. In a sense, each group seemed to have a different theory of intelligence, one group seeing it revealed in grades, another in an aptitude test. The authors were also able to show differences among the personalities of the different groups of judges. For example, Groups I and II, which emphasized grades and aptitude, tended themselves to be quite intelligent and to be low in authoritarianism. Group III, which emphasized responsibility and study habits, were less intelligent and more authoritarian than Groups I and II. Thus the research by Wiggins and her colleagues shows that individual differences in implicit personality theories can be related to the perceivers' personalities.

In summary, the idea that the perceiver has an implicit theory of personality is useful in explaining regularities in person perception. Because they have theories, people can make inferences about others from limited information. The regularities in the inferences made by various perceivers about a given individual suggest that members of a given culture share an implicit theory of personality. Finally, there is evidence to suggest that individuals have stable implicit personality theories of their own, theories which are not necessarily derived from the common culture.

Such implicit theories of personality appear to have the functional value of organizing the stimulus complex and of allowing the prediction of regularities in the behaviors of others. Since the patterns of inferences of individuals and groups of individuals can be described by a dimensional structure, the theories may consist of a series of dimensions which channel information and help form the linkages between stimulus traits and traits the perceiver infers.

Stereotypes. Implicit personality theories are, in the final analysis, stereotypes we hold about other people. A *stereotype* is a set of characteristics which is assumed to fit a category of people. We are all aware of stereotypes about Negroes, Jews, college professors, and bearded students. There is little doubt that many, perhaps most, people in our society would agree that Jews are clannish, that professors are impractical, and that bearded students are radical. For example, a classic study (Katz and Braley, 1933) showed that Princeton students had a clear consensus on which traits characterize various national groups. We remind you also that college students have stereotypes about one another (see discussion of Fink and Cantril in Chapter 1). In all fairness those stereotypes may be much less strong now than they were in the 1930's, but some data indicate that stereotypes for national groups are nearly as strong now as in the original Katz and Braley experiment (Karlins, Coffman, and Walters, 1969).

It may not have occurred to the reader that to say warm people are imaginative (as did Asch's subjects) is as much a stereotype as to say the English are sportsmanlike (as did Katz and Braley's subjects). In each case the perceiver infers something about the stimulus person which is not given directly by the information known about him.

We argued in the first chapter that stereotypes and implicit personality theories are inevitable consequences of our needs as perceivers to make sense of the world. There simply is not enough time to treat every new situation in its full particularity, nor would we be able to store the full uniqueness of each event in our memories. We are incensed about stereotypes because they imply too much about another person, and because frequently they imply negative and wrong attributes. Not all stereotypes are negative, however. The English are intelligent, the

Italians artistic, college students hardworking. These are hardly negative generalizations. We must also remember that at least some stereotypes have a basis in fact. A music lover who believes that Italians are musical may be correct if what he means is that he will be more likely to hear good opera in Milan than in Calcutta. He is, of course, wrong if he means that every Italian loves or understands opera better than every Indian. Given the capacity of most people to process information, stereotypes are inevitable, although no one would defend them as an absolute good. We should recognize them for what they are: overgeneralizations.

We need not restrict stereotypes to groups of people since it may make sense to discuss stereotypes of specific individuals. After all, if you have a good friend whom you have always seen as more athletic than intellectual, you may come to believe in that pattern of interests so strongly that you will be unable to take seriously his new interest in art history. The point is that we probably overgeneralize about the behavior of single stimulus persons over time, and this tendency also results from our need to impose stability on the behavior of others.

Acquisition of Theories of Personality

How does the individual come to have a theory of personality? This question is as broad as that which asks how people come to have stable ways of interpreting experience. Although there are no specific answers, it is likely that aspects of implicit personality theories are learned all through the socialization process. Parents may point out the joint occurrence of traits in various individuals or may often repeat such abstract phrases as "cleanliness is next to godliness." Many of the relationships between traits are probably inferred by the individual after he has noted repeated joint occurrences of characteristics in his encounters with other people; for example, he may have observed that churchgoers appear to be well scrubbed.

There seems to be some agreement within a given culture on implicit personality theories. One could take either a realist or an idealist position in explaining within-culture similarity of implicit personality theories. The realist position is that perceived relationships among traits reflect actual covariation of traits in other people. The idealist position suggests that the subjects' ratings of the traits of actual other people result primarily from the subjects' implicit theories of personality and reflect little about the traits the stimulus persons possess (Passini and Norman, 1966; Mulaik, 1964; D'Andrade, 1965). Perhaps the correspondence between our theories of personality and the actual distribution of traits among individuals in the population is zero. In some of the studies which have been cited as demonstrating that implicit theories of personality exist, the correspondence is probably quite low. In the Passini and Norman (1966) and Koltuv (1962) studies, for example, subjects assumed a high correspondence among traits for people they did not know well, and it is unlikely that these assumed relationships were based on real correspondences of traits for the particular people observed.

There may well be cultural stereotypes about the covariation of behaviors and traits which have no basis in fact. Such stereotypes are likely to be in part linguistically determined. Given that there seems to be a limited but stable number of dimensions of meaning (evaluative, activity, potency) in our culture (Osgood *et al.*, 1957), possibly we generate our personality theories by applying those dimensions of meanings of the traits. The evidence is consistent with the position that diboth reported substantial agreement between factors extracted from trait ratings of persons and factors extracted from ratings of the meaning of the traits. The evidence is consistent with the position that dimensions of meaning at least provide categories for judging others and at most determine the ways others are rated. It does not necessarily imply that judgments of others bear no relationship to the ways traits are actually related in other people.

It is conceivable that linguistic and cultural stereotypes reflect the real relationships among traits. One recent investigation gave support to this realist position. Lay and Jackson (1969) found a high correspondence between the dimensions underlying actual responses to a personality inventory and the dimensions which perceivers used in making personality ratings. There is at least some correspondence between our perceptions of trait relationships in others and the actual measured relationships between traits in others. The Lay and Jackson data dampen the criticism of those who argue that measures of implicit personality theories have been artificially produced by the meanings of the words alone.

We are impressed with the underlying thesis implicit in the research we have just discussed, namely that perceivers do develop certain rules regarding the relationships between personality characteristics. It may well be that such rules are heavily influenced by linguistic meaning although this does not appear to be the entire story. What is important is that the rules not only exist but almost certainly play a role in structuring our perceptions of other people.

PROCESSES OF IMPRESSION FORMATION

Resolution of Contradictory Information

Asch's work led to an interest not only in how inferences are drawn from partial information but also in how perceivers combine the various kinds of stimulus information to produce an impression. The emphasis here is on the stimuli and their organization. As you might expect, the question becomes most salient when the stimulus information is inconsistent, either evaluatively or logically. Given that the traits intelligent and inconsiderate are evaluatively positive and negative, respectively, we might ask how an intelligent, inconsiderate person is perceived. You may remember that Bruner *et al.* (1958) also raised that question.

Asch felt that the study of how inconsistent information is resolved would reveal something about impression formation in general. The difficulty in dealing with inconsistent information was shown very clearly in the following demonstration: One group of students (Group *A*) were asked to form an impression of a person who is intelligent-industrious-impulsive. They made their usual selection of response traits. Then they were told to form an impression of a person who is critical-stubborn-envious. After they had made their ratings, they were told that the two lists actually described a single person. Under those circumstances, subjects had great difficulties reconciling their two impressions. Group *B*, which heard only the six traits and did not make intermediate ratings, had less difficulty forming a unified impression.

Presumably there are various ways that subjects can resolve inconsistencies. An experiment by Haire and Grunes (1950) illustrates some of them. The researchers provided college students with a list of terms (e.g., reads a newspaper, cracks jokes, etc.) describing a factory worker. Some subjects were told that the worker was intelligent and some were not; intelligence as a trait was incongruent with the stereotypes of factory workers held by the majority of the subjects. The discrepant information was handled in a variety of ways. Some subjects denied the trait intelligence altogether; some denied the stimulus person's status (e.g., he was really a foreman). Other subjects tried to relate the traits in various ways to reduce inconsistencies (e.g., the worker was uneducated, he disliked office work, etc.). Other researchers (e.g., Gollin 1954; Gollin and Rosenberg, 1956; Pepitone and Hayden, 1955) have also explored the ways individuals seem to resolve inconsistencies. For our purposes it is convenient to classify them as: (a) *relational tendency*, in which either the inconsistent information is changed in meaning or new traits are inferred to relate the inconsistencies; (b) *discounting tendency*, in which part of the stimulus information is either ignored or reduced in importance; or (c) *linear combination*, in which the impression is some additive combination of the properties of the stimuli.

Order effects. One manifestation of difficulty in dealing with inconsistencies might be order effects in the presentation of information. Asch showed that when positive information about a stimulus person is presented before negative information, the general impression is more positive than it is when the reverse order is used. A *primacy effect* occurs when information presented first is more influential in determining the final impression. An experiment by Luchins (1957a) illustrates the general phenomenon. Luchins presented subjects with two one-paragraph descriptions of a stimulus person, Jim. One paragraph described Jim as friendly, outgoing, and extroverted (*E*), and the other as shy and introverted (*I*). Subjects rating the two paragraphs separately did indeed see Jim-*E* as more friendly than Jim-*I*. The question asked by Luchins was to what extent subjects who read both paragraphs would have their overall impressions affected by the order of the paragraphs. Would subjects who read them in an *E–I* order see Jim as more friendly than would subjects who read them in an *I–E* order? Luchins, like Asch, found that the information read first had the more powerful impact: subjects who read the paragraphs in the *E–I* order did see Jim as more friendly than subjects who read them in the *I–E* order.

In the last section we suggested three general mechanisms for dealing with inconsistencies: relational tendency, discounting tendency, and linear combination. Asch clearly favored the first. He argued that the first information sets up a directional tendency to which later information is assimilated.

> When the subject hears the first term, a broad, uncrystallized but directed impression is born. The next characteristic comes not as a separate item, but is related to the established direction. Quickly the view formed acquires a certain stability, so that later characteristics are fitted—if conditions permit—to the given direction.*

Luchins (1957b) gives a similar argument in terms of set, or *Einstellung*. In the typical *Einstellung* experiment subjects solve a number of problems with a common strategy. They are then presented with a problem which can be solved with the previous strategy but can be dealt with more efficiently by the use of a new and simpler strategy. Under these circumstances many subjects persist with the old strategy, thus demonstrating the effects of the previous set. In the same vein, the first information in the impression-formation task may act to create a set which determines the way the final information is interpreted.

One could argue that new information is inferred which helps relate the inconsistencies. Suppose that you receive information first that a person is *kind* and then that he is *dishonest*. You might infer that he is a modern Robin Hood who steals to help the sick and needy. In a sense, the person is basically seen as kind, and his dishonesty is somewhat

---

*S. E. Asch, "Forming impressions of personality," *Journal of Abnormal and Social Psychology*, 1946, **41**, 271–272.

subordinate. On the other hand, you might assume that the stimulus person is a con-man whose kindness is subordinate to his more basic dishonesty.

A second possibility (and the one seemingly favored by Asch) is that the terms actually change meaning in relation to one another. Surely the neuroticism of a great author or painter is of a quality different from the neuroticism of your neighbor. For the former, having a messy room is creative eccentricity; for the latter, sloppiness. It is, of course, hard to measure changes in meaning or, for that matter, the meanings of words themselves. What evidence we do have (Anderson, 1966; Anderson and Lampel, 1965; Wyer and Dermer, 1968) suggests that evaluations of individual traits change as a function of their context. The trait "kind" is evaluated more positively alone than when it appears in the triad dishonest-kind-ugly. Strangely enough, it is not necessary that the perceiver feel that the trait and the context traits belong to the same individual to get the effect although it is necessary that he consider the traits collectively (Wyer and Dermer, 1968). Many explanations of context effects on the evaluation of traits are possible; some recent evidence has been interpreted as indicating shifts of meaning (Wyer and Watson, 1969).

Assuming a discounting mechanism is an alternative way of explaining primacy effects. In the first demonstration of this in the context of impression formation, Dailey (1952) was able to show that subjects who had formed impressions about another did not deal effectively with information presented later. Anderson and Jacobson (1965) found small but reliable tendencies for subjects to reduce the weight or importance of information inconsistent with the bulk of evidence presented about a stimulus person. So the primacy effect may be grounded in tendencies to ignore, deny, supress, or forget the later information which is inconsistent with the previous information.

There have been attempts to test directly whether relational tendencies or discounting tendencies account for primacy effects. Anderson and Hubert (1963) obtained evidence that when subjects are told that they will be asked to recall the stimulus adjectives presented (thus presumably ensuring adequate attention to the later adjectives), not only does the primacy effect disappear but a slight *recency effect* occurs. In a related experiment Stewart (1965) reasoned that asking subjects to form an impression for each new piece of information should force them to pay attention to all pieces of information. Subjects who were so instructed showed a slight recency effect. Given that forced attention to all the stimulus traits seems to eliminate the primacy effect, it can easily be argued that the primacy effect may result from lack of attention to or reduction in importance of the later, inconsistent adjectives.

Various other researchers (e.g., Luchins, 1958; Rosenkrantz and Crockett, 1965) obtained recency effects when the subject was asked to form an impression after the first block of information (whether positive or negative) and again after the second block (of opposite valence). While it is not clear why writing an impression after the first block of information should produce recency effects, it is possible the subject feels that, having formally dealt with the first information, he should now give close attention to the second block of information. In a sense, the mere fact that he has processed the first information successfully makes more salient the need to deal equally well with the second block, and that need leads to a discounting of the information presented first.

Variables of other kinds may influence tendencies to discount part of the stimulus information. One might be the perceiver's expectation of how he will use the information he has about another. Zajonc's (1960) theory of cognitive tuning argued that a person who expected to transmit a message to another would have a more rigid and polarized cognitive orientation toward the material, whereas a person who did not expect to have to transmit information should be prepared for any kind of material, and his cognitive structure would be more flexible.

Cohen (1961) applied that model to impression formation. Subjects were asked to form an impression of a person described by 10 moderately or highly contradictory traits. Some subjects believed they would have to transmit their impressions to others while other subjects believed they would receive another's message about his impression. As predicted, subjects in the transmission condition were inclined to suppress contradictory elements in their impressions and to polarize their evaluations of the stimulus person. Leventhal (1962) also found evidence consistent with Zajonc's theory.

The evidence we have reviewed thus far seems to indicate that when there are inconsistencies among stimuli, part of the stimulus information is discounted, ignored, or reduced in importance. There is also evidence to suggest that shifts in meaning do occur under certain circumstances.

Combining evaluative characteristics. The third hypothesis, linear combination, has been most commonly applied to evaluative consistencies. While inconsistencies among stimulus traits could presumably be of various kinds, researchers have tended to concentrate on evaluative conflict. Many researchers feel that the evaluative response to another person is fundamental and accounts for a substantial portion of the rating variance. Empirically, an evaluative dimension nearly always accounts for a large share of the rating variance of both objects and people (Osgood *et al.*, 1957; Warr and Knapper, 1968; Frijda, 1969). Frequently that share of the variance is more than two-thirds of the total; halo effects are pervasive in ratings of others. It is also clear that the evaluative dimension has great relevance for our behavior toward a stimulus person. Typically, we would expect to interact in different ways and to different extents with liked versus disliked others.

Various models have been proposed to account for the evaluation of the total impression as a function of its component traits. Several general additive models have been considered very seriously. By an additive model we mean one in which the final evaluation (E) is some linear function of the evaluations of each individual trait (S). Remember that Asch had specifically attacked an additive model and had said that the final impression was not an additive function of the component traits. We are now suggesting that the *evaluation* of the final impression may well be a linear function of the *evaluations* of the component traits. In order to test this hypothesis, we will need to present subjects with a list of traits, and we will have to know how positively or negatively subjects in general (or our individual subjects) have rated each of the traits. We can ask the subject how positively he would feel toward a person described by those traits, and we can then determine how adequately his final evaluation can be predicted from a knowledge of how positively he evaluates the component traits. Almost all the research reviewed in this section uses some variant of that method.

The two simplest models are the *summation* and the *averaging* models. Triandis and Fishbein (1963) proposed the *summation* model to account for the evaluation of variations in race, occupation, nationality, and religion. The question was how the subject evaluated various stimulus persons, e.g., a *white French bank manager of the same religion as the subject* or a *Negro Portuguese coal miner of a different religion.* Triandis and Fishbein found that the model which best predicted the evaluation of such combinations was one in which the final evaluation was simply the sum of the evaluation of the components,

$$E = \Sigma S_k,$$

where S_k represents the evaluation of each component.

Various *averaging* models have been used. All such models predict that the final evaluation is a function of the average evaluation of the stimuli. A simple averaging model (Anderson, 1962) assumes that all stimuli are equally weighted, and the simple average is taken:

$$E = \frac{\Sigma S_k}{N},$$

where E is the final evaluation, S_k represents the evaluation of each stimulus trait, and N is the number of traits. More complex averaging models assign different weights to the stimuli so that the stimuli contribute unequally to the final impression (Osgood and Tannenbaum,

1955; Anderson, 1968b). Weighted-average models are a bit like courses in which final grades are calculated on the basis of different weights for different examinations. For example, the final exam might be weighted twice as heavily as a midterm in calculating the final grade. We will later suggest some uses of such a weighted-average model in impression formation, but first we should explore an important difference between summation models on the one hand and averaging models (whether the average is simple or weighted) on the other.

We should emphasize that the *summation* and *averaging* models both have a simple additive basis but that under some circumstances they imply different things. Let us suppose that subjects are presented with some or all of the following stimulus traits with their evaluations (on a 10-point scale) in parentheses: moral (10), bold (6), happy (8), industrious (6). Group *A* are given moral, happy, and industrious; Group *B*, moral, bold, happy, and industrious. The summation model predicts that Group *B* will have the more favorable final evaluation since their total amount of positive information is greater, whereas the simple averaging model says that Group *A* will see the stimulus person more favorably because the Group *A* traits produce a higher average evaluation.

Group *A*			Group *B*		
S_1	moral	10	S_1	moral	10
S_2	happy	8	S_2	happy	8
S_3	industrious	6	S_3	industrious	6
			S_4	bold	6
$\Sigma S_k =$		24	$\Sigma S_k =$		30
$\frac{\Sigma S_k}{N} =$		8.0	$\frac{\Sigma S_k}{N} =$		7.50

The difference between the two models is not trivial. The first implies that the way to obtain a more favorable evaluation is to keep adding favorable traits; the second says that the traits added must be more favorable than the existing average. In the summation model, adding a moderately positive trait would increase the evaluation, but in the averaging model, adding such a trait would decrease it.

Since Anderson (1968a) his scaled over 500 trait names on an evaluative scale, it is now relatively easy to compare the models directly; and as one might expect, research has refined them. Anderson (1965) did a systematic study, varying the number, quality, and mix of the stimuli. A subject got either two or four traits as stimuli; there were four levels of favorability (L, $M-$, $M+$, H) in the several groups of stimuli; and the two or four stimuli presented to a subject were either uniformly of one type or varied. The averaging model predicts that adding moderately positive stimuli ($M+$) to highly positive stimuli (H) will lower the final evaluation because the average of the set will decrease; the summation model predicts that the larger set will be more positively evaluated because of the greater quantity of positive information. The data show that evaluations of an $H\ H\ M+\ M+$ set are lower than those of an $H\ H$ set, thus supporting the averaging model. However, an $H\ H\ H\ H$ stimulus person is evaluated more positively than an $H\ H$ stimulus person—a result that does not fit a simple ($E = \Sigma S_k/N$) averaging model since the average of four highly favorable stimuli is presumably the same as two.

Anderson developed a weighted-average formula to account for this effect. The *weighted-average* model assumes, in essence, that the subject begins with a neutral impression, which is averaged upward by positive stimuli and downward by negative stimuli. The greater the number of consistently positive or negative stimuli, the larger the average will be.*

There may be some confusion about the psychological meaning of S_0, the so-called initial impression. It may be considered a kind of general bias which the judge has in his ratings. It indicates the "empty" impression he would have of a stimulus person if no information were provided and as such it takes account of the fact that extreme general evaluative ratings are hard to achieve; such ratings are always dampened by the tendency to begin with a neutral impression.

The general equation can easily be modified to take account of differences in S values among stimuli and differences in weight among stimuli. If we want to account for primacy effects in impression formation, for example, it may be convenient to assume decreasing weight for later stimuli. It can simply be assumed that any factor which decreases the salience of any stimulus trait (by discounting later traits, for example) will also decrease their weight. In recent research efforts (e.g., Anderson, 1965; Anderson and Jacobson, 1965), the averaging

---

*The formula is

$$E = \frac{nwS + (1 - w)\,S_0}{nw + (1 - w)},$$

where n is the number of traits, w is the weight assigned to each stimulus trait, S is the scale value of each trait, and S_0 is some initial (neutral) impression. Assume that each trait has the same weight and evaluative rating. The formula can of course be modified to deal with situations in which the weights and evaluative ratings differ.

model has provided a good fit for trait data in impression-formation tasks.

We have discussed various processes by which perceivers resolve inconsistent information about a stimulus person. Since words are not precise in their meanings and therefore depend in part on their context for meaning, inconsistencies can be resolved through shifts in meanings of inconsistent traits. The kindness of a mother and the kindness of an ingratiator are not the same. Probably because meaning is so hard to measure, relatively little empirical knowledge is available about this mode of processing information about others. On the other hand, there is considerable evidence in support of both discounting and linear combination (whether averaging or summation) as frequently used processes in impression formation. Relatively little attention has been paid to the factors determining when a perceiver will form a consistent impression by discounting part of the inconsistent information, by taking its average or sum, or by attempting to change the meaning of one or more pieces of information. Our best present guess is that all three mechanisms are used from time to time.

Individual differences in dealing with inconsistent information. One real possibility is that different people prefer to use different strategies in reconciling inconsistencies. There may be averagers and discounters. Recently some researchers have tried to relate the individual's way of resolving inconsistent information to his personality and information-processing style. Of the wealth of personality variables available, two have been most often used: authoritarianism and cognitive complexity.

The authoritarian person (as measured by the *F*-Scale, Adorno *et al.*, 1950) is hypothesized to have a trait cluster, or syndrome, which includes a desire for structured social relationships with clear authority ranks, prejudices against and dislike of unknown or "foreign" people (*ethnocentrism*), intolerance of ambiguous situations, desires for cognitive and affective clarity. We may summarize the syndrome by saying that authoritarians are people whose needs for certainty lead them to avoid or dislike potentially inconsistent information and who adopt rather simple modes of processing information (see Byrne, 1966, for a short introduction to the literature on authoritarianism.)

Steiner (1954) argued that ethnocentrism (dislike and fear of people in other groups), which conceptually and empirically bears a close relationship to authoritarianism, should be related to sensitivity to evaluative inconsistency of traits. Specifically, high-ethnocentric subjects may feel that the same person cannot possess both positive and negative traits, but low-ethnocentric subjects would probably feel much less uncomfortable with such discrepancies. Steiner showed that high-ethnocentric subjects were less likely to see evaluatively discrepant traits as going together than were low-ethnocentric subjects.

Steiner and Johnson (1963) were able to demonstrate a low but significant ($r = .26$) correlation between the full *F*-scale and intolerance of trait inconsistency. Warr and Sims (1965) found that high authoritarians are more likely to see evaluatively similar traits as going together. Thus it seems likely that authoritarian people are particularly upset by evaluative inconsistencies.

In general, evidence favors the proposition that authoritarians seem to be pushed to form unambiguous, evaluatively consistent impressions. Perhaps they achieve such clarity by ignoring or suppressing part of the inconsistent data although the evidence is weak on the issue.

Another important personality variable which has a theoretical relationship to ways of resolving contradictory information is cognitive complexity. Actually, cognitive complexity can be seen as related to authoritarianism although the two variables are measured quite differently and come from two different traditions in psychology. Kelly (1955), Witkin *et al.* (1962), Harvey, Hunt, and Schroder (1961), and Schroder, Driver, and Streufert (1967) have built personality models around the notions of cognitive complexity and differentiation.

While there are significant disagreements among researchers as to the definition and measurement of cognitive complexity, nearly everyone agrees that the cognitively complex person has more categories and makes more distinctions in his perceptions. One implication of this view is that the cognitively simple person will be likely to rate others as extreme because he has fewer categories of judgment. In the extreme case he may use only one dimension (good-bad) and be able to place others into only one or the other of those categories. The complex person has more dimensions and can presumably make finer discriminations along each dimension. Although our hypothetical extremely simple judge can label people only as good or bad, a more complex judge can say not only that a stimulus person is a little or a lot good or bad, but also that he is kind or unkind, happy or sad, etc. Scott (1963) and Supnick (quoted in Crockett, 1965) found that complex subjects were less likely than simple ones to see the world in dichotomized terms. For example, Supnick showed that in written descriptions of others, cognitively simple subjects were more inclined to describe the other as either completely favorable or unfavorable. Perhaps the cognitively complex subjects have a greater capacity to tolerate contradictory information about a single person (Crockett, 1965). The cognitively complex person appears to be able to live with the fact that people can be contradictory—that, for example, an honest person on occasion can do an unkind thing or can be ingratiating.

How well do cognitively complex and simple subjects integrate contradictory information about others into their impressions? One line of research on this problem was conducted by Crockett (Mayo and Crockett, 1964; Rosenkrantz and Crockett, 1965). He has suggested that the recency effects described by Luchins (1957b) might be accounted for primarily by the low-complexity subjects. Recall that Luchins had subjects form impressions after each of two contradictory blocks of information had been presented, and he found that the later information tended to predominate in the final impression. The argument is that cognitively complex people have a differentiation of traits, a subtlety of relationships among traits, and a tolerance for contradictory information not possessed by the cognitively simple subjects. It might be said that cognitively simple people have rigid, brittle structures which must give way under the force of competing information, and that complex people have more resilient structures. Thus the complex people would be able to incorporate the disconfirming evidence into a modified structure, but the simple people would be more inclined to discount the first impression (which is destroyed by the second, contradictory information) and to build a new impression around the second information. Mayo and Crockett (1964) found that the cognitively simple subjects showed large recency effects. They reacted to favorable information with very favorable impressions and then, when presented later with negative information, became quite negative in their impressions. The cognitively complex subjects, on the other hand, became less extreme when they encountered the new information and achieved a final impression which was a balance of the two kinds of information. Leventhal and Singer (1964) also reported data which showed that cognitively simple judges changed more with disconfirming evidence, but more recently Rosenkrantz and Crockett (1965) have reported data not completely in line with the hypothesis.

Although the evidence is not completely clear, it is consistent with the proposition that high authoritarians and cognitively simple subjects are inclined to form simple and evaluatively unambiguous impressions of other people. We hypothesize that they employ discounting as the mechanism for dealing with inconsistent information but that low authoritarians and cognitively complex subjects are more likely to use relational mechanisms and linear combinations.

In this section we have attempted to treat some representative data on individual differences in processing information about others. We have speculated (although the supporting data are either lacking or weak and conflicting) that some kinds of people are more likely to use suppression and discounting mechanisms and others are probably more inclined to use relational strategies. Gollin (1954, and with Rosenberg, 1956) showed that different subjects do use different strategies, and we have tried to isolate two major dimensions of personality, authoritarianism and cognitive complexity, which may be related to those different tendencies.

The fact that individual differences exist should not, of course, reduce our confidence that certain general processes also occur in impression formation. Under some circumstances, almost all people may form impressions in the same way; nonetheless, under other circumstances, individual perceivers may have maximum freedom to form impressions in their own ways.

WHERE IS THE PERSON?

One might have the idea that somehow the stimulus person has been lost in a welter of traits, dimensions, and verbal garbage. Do all these results say anything about the perception of people? This question was initially asked of the Asch experiments by Luchins (1948), but Kelley (1950) provided data based on perceptions of real people which supported Asch's results. Furthermore, in a number of the experiments we have reviewed (e.g., Cronbach, 1955; Koltuv, 1962), subjects rated real people known to them. It has also been shown (e.g., Warr and Knapper, 1968) that the Asch results can be replicated, using narrative descriptions of stimulus persons rather than trait names. Thus there is every reason to believe that Asch's paradigm is a valuable, albeit simplified, tool for studying the way we organize information about others.

A more basic point is simply that, to the extent that we assign to people traits based on observations of their behavior or on hearsay, this research has a great deal to say about other inferences we make. Bruner *et al.* (1958) suggested that impression formation was concerned with how we form concepts about others based on partial information. Inference processes are part of that game, and since we rarely, if ever, have complete information about others, it is important to study how the missing data are supplied.

Finally, we should point out that there is nothing magical about the traits we assign to others. Traits are our way of packaging the behavior of others. Our discussion in Chapter 1 of three levels of experience should remind you that, in moving from feelings to descriptions of behavior to descriptions of the personality characteristics of others, we are treating increasingly more abstract experience.

It is indeed possible that kindness, say, does not exist in some fundamental fashion. As a matter of cultural and linguistic convenience, we call certain behaviors kind and say that a person is kind or unkind. Perhaps all we really have is a set of linguistic labels, as well as a set of conventions for applying them to people. If that is true—there is disagreement on this point; the reader may wish to compare Allport (1961) and Mischel (1968)—then the study of how our linguistic labels are organized and how that organization determines and is determined by the conventions of application is absolutely appropriate and fundamental.

In the final analysis, impression formation is the study of cognitive processes as applied to perception of people. We have yet to see any data on impression formation which cannot be subsumed under more general cognitive processes. Of course, the truism that people are frustratingly complex stimulus objects makes the process complicated to study. Nonetheless, we persist in maintaining the belief that the study of impression formation both adds to and is added to by the study of cognitive processes.

CHAPTER FOUR

Attribution Theory

We have considered our ability to assess the emotional states and personality characteristics of others, and we have tried to describe the processes by which we use our knowledge of some characteristics of the person to infer others. For the most part, however, we have been dealing with abstract representations of the other person—photographs, traits, etc.; we have not yet considered the other as we usually come to know him in real life, as an active participant with us in social interactions. In this chapter we shall be concerned with analyzing the processes by which we infer dispositional properties of another person from our observations of his behavior in social situations.

THE PHENOMENOLOGY OF SOCIAL BEHAVIOR

The major impetus to research in the area of social behavior phenomenology was the theoretical analysis of Fritz Heider as presented initially in his paper on phenomenal causality (1944) and elaborated in *The Psychology of Interpersonal Relations* (1958). Heider begins with three fundamental assumptions. The first is that adequate understanding of people's social behavior rests on a description of how they perceive and report their social world. Heider calls his psychology naive because it is based on the phenomenology of the average person and it relies heavily on common-sense language for describing person perception. Second, he assumes that people desire to predict and control their environments. People want to be able to anticipate the effects their behavior will have on the environment and on themselves. They also would like to be able to structure their worlds so as to produce favorable outcomes, and their success rests, of course, on their ability to predict. Third, Heider believes that there are basic similarities between object and person perception, and that the process of predicting the physical environment does not differ in kind from the process of predicting the behavior of others. The social world may be less predictable than the physical, but what predictability there is in the social world is achieved by the same processes that are involved in perception of the physical world.

Heider relies on a model of perception developed by Egon Brunswik (1956) and usually called probabilistic functionalism. Brunswik saw the fundamental problem of perception as the coordination of perceptions with objects. Given that conscious experiences are always mediated by the environment and the physiology of the perceiver, how are we able to sort out the "true" object and its characteristics? To put it differently, how are we able to perceive the characteristics of an object despite wide variability in the environmental conditions under which it is perceived? We considered this problem under "stability" in Chapter I when we discussed the constancies in perception and introduced the concept of invariance. The retinal size of an object varies widely as it or we move about, yet we perceive object size to be constant because we take the distance from object to retina into account; our perception is determined by our application of the invariance between retinal size, and actual object size and distance.

Heider argues that in person perception a similar problem exists. If the enduring or dispositional properties, e.g., friendliness, which we attempt to attribute to others were perfectly coordinated with a particular kind of behavior, there would be no problem. If there were a finite number of friendly behaviors which could be manifestations only of friendliness and of nothing else, the attribution would be determined. But just as retinal size is only probabilistically related to object size, so a given behavior is only probabilistically related to a given personality trait. The example shown in Fig. 4.1 serves to illustrate the problem.

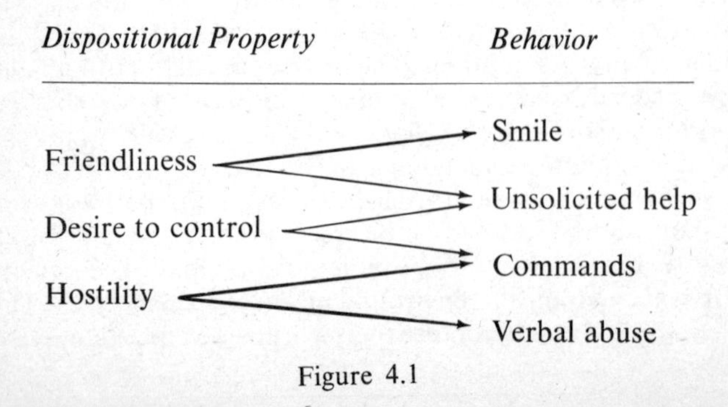

Figure 4.1

Helping behavior may be coordinated either with friendliness or with desire to control, and the attribution you choose will probably make a difference. You will predict quite different ultimate outcomes from interacting with a person who wants to control you and with another who is friendly. The point of this discussion is that behaviors are rarely if ever coordinated with one and only one dispositional property. Nevertheless, we do perceive stability in this complex, indeterminate environment of other people by making inferences about the other person's motives and dispositions. Heider's analysis represents an attempt to deal systematically with the conditions which affect the inference process.

The perception of causality. Central to Heider's entire theoretical position is the proposition that man perceives behavior as being caused, and that the causal locus can be either in the perceiver or in the environment. Correctly or incorrectly, people are perceived as loci of causality: most of us feel we control and determine at least part of our actions, and we perceive others to have similar powers. In this most general of attribution processes, man acts as a scientist in attempting to find sufficient and necessary reasons for the occurrence of a particular behavior; he seeks the cause of the event to enable him to predict future events. The perception of causality has been of interest to more than a few psychologists.

In a recent contribution to motivation theory, deCharms, for example, states that "*Man's primary motivation propensity is to be effective in producing changes in his environment*. Man strives to be a causal agent. . . . "* He suggests, moreover, that the roots of the perception of causality lie in the individual's experiences of efficacy vis-à-vis the environment, his awareness that variations in his behavior produce variations in environmental effects. If this were true, the perception of others as causal agents would result from generalization, and variations in a person's experiences of efficacy would produce variations in the extent to which he considers another person to be the origin of his own actions or to be a pawn of the environment.

The Belgian psychologist Michotte (1963) reports a number of simple experiments which show that people immediately perceive causality. A small object, *A*, glides along and touches a stationary object, *B*. *A* stops and *B* immediately begins moving in the direction *A* would have taken. In this situation subjects say that *A* pushed *B* or caused *B* to move. If, on the other hand, the movement of *B* is delayed for a brief time (more than 0.2 seconds) after *A* strikes it, the perception of causality is destroyed. From this small demonstration we can at least say that subjects have a bias toward using causal language; moreover, there is

---

*Richard deCharms, *Personal Causation* (New York: Academic Press, 1968), p. 269; italics in the original.

every evidence that the perception of causality in this situation is direct and immediate. Heider and Simmel (1944) demonstrated similar effects when subjects viewed a short movie of one large and two small geometric figures moving about a boxlike structure with a "door" in it. In one sequence subjects perceived the larger shape to be "chasing" the smaller ones, thus causing them to flee; and they often attributed dispositional characteristics to the shapes. For example, the large figure was seen as a bully.

The hypothesis that we are "biased" toward causal perceptions because of our own feelings of causal efficacy received support from studies by Jean Piaget (1930) on the development of causal thinking in children. The most general interpretation of his work is that, by the age at which a child can answer an examiner's questions, the idea of causality is already firmly fixed and that the subsequent course of development is toward a more sophisticated and less universal sense of causality. Initially, the child simply assumes that two related events have a causal connection; he seems unaware that other possibilities exist. The concept of causation may well develop from the experience of the child, who is learning to manipulate the physical objects in his world; his sense of efficacy or power is translated into causal perceptions. When the child moves a block, he is aware of the results of his behavior. In some sense he knows he caused the block to move. Given the young child's tendency to overgeneralize or to accomodate new data to existing schemata, it is not surprising that the majority of changes in the environment are perceived as caused, since the first changes cognized by the child were, in fact, caused by him.

If we can assume that perceivers tend to perceive events as caused, we may then ask about the dimensions of causal attribution. One central distinction is attribution to the person, on the one hand, or to the environment, on the other, i.e., the distinction between the perception of internal or external causality (e.g., Thibaut and Riecken, 1955) or of people as origins or pawns (deCharms, 1968).

Presumably the outcomes of action are caused by some combination of personal characteristics and environmental forces. The person may have done something because he had to do it, the environmental forces being unusually strong; or because he wanted to do it, internal dispositional properties being strong enough to cause the behavior within the existing environment. In Heider's analysis an action outcome or effect is perceived to be an additive function of the effective environmental force and the effective person force, which is in turn a multiplicative function of the other's power or ability and the effort he exerts (referred to as trying).

$$\text{Effect} = f\,[\text{Environmental force} + \text{Personal force}\ (\text{Ability} \times \text{Trying})]$$

The additive relationship between environmental and personal force implies one of three things: environmental force or personal force could produce the action outcome if the other were absent (either a man with a rake or a strong wind could remove leaves from a lawn); the environmental force could work toward the same end as the personal force and thus supplement it; or the environmental force could work to oppose the personal force and thus reduce its effectiveness. The multiplicative relationship between power and trying, on the other hand, implies that if either component were absent, the strength of the personal force would be zero. A person could try very hard to produce an event, but if he had no power, the exertion would come to naught. Likewise, power becomes a force only when effort is exerted. In order to make an attribution of internal or external causality, the perceiver must estimate the relative strengths of the environmental and personal forces. One of the most important decisions the perceiver makes is his estimate of the extent to which the internal rather than the environmental force (including other people) was responsible for the effects of a person's actions.

Heider also divides perceptions of causality into instances of personal causality and impersonal causality. Perceived personal causality is a subset of perceived internal causality and encompasses only those events which the other intended to produce. Impersonal causality consists not only of externally caused effects but also of effects which were caused by the other but which he did not try to cause. The latter might occur if there was some accidental or unforeseen effect of behavior, such as having a flat tire on the way to an appointment. The person intended to be on time and did not intend to have the flat tire. Personal causation of a given effect, on the other hand, requires that the person have the ability to create the effect and have tried to create that effect. The personal-impersonal distinction is central to Heider's analysis in that the person is held responsible only for personally caused effects, and in that only such effects are usually informative about dispositional properties of the person. What I try to do and have the ability to do may reveal something about the inner me, but accidental and unforeseen consequences of my behavior say little or nothing about my enduring dispositional properties. We will now take up in greater detail a theoretical discussion of the perception of the effective personal forces.

The perception of can. Can is a dispositional property which refers to a relationship between ability and environment. A person may have high ability (be strong), but because the environmental forces are also strong (a house weighs many tons), he may not be able to perform certain tasks (lifting the house). So the *can* factor has an internal component, ability, and an external component, environmental obstacles. Before attributions of *can* are made, we must know something about the environment. There are also dispositional qualities to the environment, one of the most important of which is difficulty. Tasks are judged as to how easy or hard they are. If a task is extremely easy, then virtually no ability is required to perform it; on the other hand, if a task is extremely difficult, so much ability is required that we say no one can do it. Therefore, extremely easy or difficult environments make attributions of *can* trivial. Maximum information about differential abilities is most clearly provided by behavior on tasks of moderate difficulty. Some people will be able to do them and others will not. If a person does perform a moderately difficult task, we have rather clear evidence that he can do it, unless we have reason to believe environmental factors like "luck" have entered in; if he fails at such a task, however, we have less clear evidence about ability since it is possible he had the ability and did not try. Thus certain outcomes of our naive experiments are more informative than others. It is probably true that "nothing speaks louder than success," and if anything, most people are inclined to over-attribute ability based on success.

The perception of trying. In the naive analysis of action, perception of trying has two components: intention and exertion. The first refers to *what* a person wants to do (not *why* he wants to do it) and the second to how hard he tries to do it. When a professor says a student is trying in a course, he usually means both that the student wants to do well (i.e., learn the material and/or get a good grade) and that he is working hard by doing the reading carefully and attending class regularly. Exertion is coordinated with the person's abilities and with environmental difficulty. A person of low ability must work harder on a given task than a person of high ability; difficult tasks require greater trying than easier ones. Heider does not discuss perceptions of exertion in great detail probably because how hard a person works is often obvious; sweat and hours are good metrics for exertion.

Perceptions of what a person wants to do are not so immediately apparent because of the existence of *equifinality*, which in Heider's system refers to the existence of a number of paths to the same goal. What the person wants to do may be fixed, but he has a number of means to achieve his aim. If someone wishes to demonstrate his friendliness, he may greet you warmly and engage in conversation when he meets you on the street, invite you to dinner, and send you a card on your birthday. If things go as he plans, you may infer that he is friendly toward you or is a friendly person. At the same time, a given action usually accomplishes several things. By talking with you on the street, he may make you late for class, anger some other person who wants his or your attention, block traffic, etc. The latter effects were unintended, and the perceiver must determine which of the effects of an action were intended in order to make dispositional inferences about the other person. As an exercise in person perception, the reader might want to think about one of his own recent behaviors and ask himself what unintended effects it could have had. From the perspective of a perceiver, the effects you did intend to produce may not have been clear. Some cues we use in estimating whether or not the person is trying to produce a given effect are his verbal statement of his goals, the extent to which he seems to be exerting himself, and his behavior when his actions are thwarted. In the latter instance, if he attempts to avoid the encountered obstacle or engages in several behaviors which lead to the same apparent goal, we infer that he is trying to reach that goal.

In his discussion of how people analyze action, Heider points to variables which are important determinants of our attributions of dispositional properties to others. We take into account information regarding the strength of environmental forces in deciding whether or not the other caused the effects, and we then infer both how able he is and how hard he was trying. Heider focuses attention on the distinctions between internal and external causality, personal and impersonal causality, and on the fact that our perceptions regarding *can* and *try* determine to a great extent the attribution of both intent and dispositional properties to others. Heider's discussion, however, cannot be considered a systematic theory which makes concrete, unequivocal predictions for actual situations. There have been two major attempts to rectify this situation; the first was presented by Jones and Davis (1965) in their paper "From Acts to Dispositions" and the second by Kelley (1967) in "Attribution Theory in Social Psychology." We shall focus our attention on the Jones and Davis analysis primarily because they concentrate more heavily on explicating Heider's analysis of person perception. Kelley's very important paper pushes in the direction of generalizing the position to other areas of social psychology and making attribution the central process in social interaction. Kelley's paper is strongly recommended to anyone interested in the attribution process.

THE ACT TO DISPOSITIONAL MODEL

The Jones and Davis (1965) attribution analysis makes some simplifying assumptions in the basic Heider model. Like Heider's model, it assumes that behavior has effects and that the perceiver attempts to account for the causes of behavior in terms of the effects. Behavior is accounted for to the extent that it can be related to the personal disposition of the person perceived or to the environment; Jones and Davis concern themselves only with attribution to the person. Thus they are concerned primarily with internal causality. They also simplify Heider's discussion by assuming that the actor was aware of what effects would result from his action and that he had the ability to create those effects. The perceiver then tries to infer what effects the actor intended to create, and under certain conditions those intentions are used to infer dispositional properties of the person.

The authors introduce the term *correspondence* to describe the extent to which (1) a given intention can describe the action, (2) a given dispositional property can account for the intention, and (3) by implication, a given dispositional property can describe the action. In general, an inference is correspondent to the extent that the same or similar words describe the behavior and its underlying cause. You compliment a hostess' dinner because you want to or intend to win her approval, i.e., because you have a high need for approval. You behave in an unpleasant manner because you are a hostile person. Correspondent inferences are more extreme and more certain. The inference "he is a very warm person" is more correspondent than "he is a fairly warm person." Because extremeness of rating is highly correlated with confidence of rating (Green, 1954), extreme attributions are likely to be made more confidently. Correspondence of inferences is assumed to vary inversely with the social desirability and the number of noncommon effects of the behavior and directly with the hedonic relevance and inferred personalism of the behavior and its effects. We will consider these variables in turn.

The variable of *social desirability* has two functions for Jones and Davis. In the first place, it is assumed that people intend desirable effects from their action. A night on the town may have the effects of providing me with a good time, reducing my bank account, and giving me a hangover. Presumably I intended the first effect and not the other two. Second, socially desirable effects provide little information about the distinctiveness of people.

By social desirability of effects in this context, Jones and Davis really mean how usual or "normal" the effects are. If a person performs a socially desirable, expected act, we have little evidence about him except that he is similar to most other people. For example, if a friend asked for a loan of a dollar and it was granted, we would not be prepared to say that the lender is particularly kind or helpful. Since most people would have done the same thing, he could simply have been responding to a norm about granting small loans to friends. We cannot tell whether his behavior was caused by his generosity or by his adherence to social norms (internally or externally caused). If he had refused to grant the loan (when he had money, i.e., the ability to grant the request), we would be more likely to say that he is unkind, stingy, or something of the sort because his behavior was unusual. So the simple rule is that as the effects of behavior deviate more markedly from what the average person would do or norms say he should do, we can infer more about him and our attributions become more correspondent. All other things being equal, we would feel more confident saying a man is generous if he has given $500 to someone in need than if he has run a short errand for a friend, and more altruistic in the latter case than if he has lent 50 cents to a friend. But there are problems even with these examples because in each case forces other than generosity, e.g., a high need for approval, could have produced the same behavior. For example, since generosity is socially approved, the person who gives $500 to another may simply have a higher need for approval than the person who lends 50 cents. Jones and Davis discuss this problem of interpretation under the rubric of noncommon effects.

Implicit in the analysis regarding noncommon effects is the assumption that the actor is observed performing several actions or that his action is a conscious decision in the light of known alternative courses of action. In the former case we search for the common effects of the several behaviors. In each of the examples cited above, intentions other than a desire to help may be operating. One effect of each of those actions is to gain approval from another. For example, an altruistic act has (for simplicity's sake) two effects: helping another and winning his approval. Before I can attribute the helping action to altruism or to need for approval, I must know which effect was intended. This is where the variable of noncommon effects enters. You observe that I run several errands for a friend who is sick, and that I make an anonymous gift of $500 to my alma mater. The first act could be motivated by altruism and by a need for approval; the second by altruism and the desire to reduce my income taxes. The effect common to the two actions is aid to another person; approval and income tax relief are noncommon effects. Surely, then, I am an altruistic person. When a perceiver observes only a single behavior of another person and its many effects, it may help him to compare the effects of the chosen behavior with the effects of several rejected behaviors. A friend chooses to go to a college which is near his home, has a good academic reputation, is small and coed. He rejects a college which is 500 miles away, has a good academic reputation, is small and coed. You can be reasonably certain that the friend's choice is based on the noncommon effect of distance, and you might infer that he is dependent on his parents or perhaps that he does not want to leave a high school sweetheart. Thus correspondence, the certainty with which we make inferences about intentions and dispositions, increases as the social desirability of effects decreases and as the number of noncommon effects between the given action and a nonchosen action decreases.

Correspondence varies directly with the personal involvement of the perceiver in the effects of the other's action. *Hedonic relevance* refers to the extent that a person's action proves rewarding or costly to the perceiver. Jones and Davis admit that it is not quite clear why this variable should increase correspondence; they speculate, however, that as relevance increases, several effects will be grouped together under the rubric most relevant to the given perceiver, and hence the number of noncommon effects will be reduced. If one of your actions is relevant to one of my values (you have, say, violated standards of academic integrity), then I may come to see several of the effects of your actions as indicating dishonesty. In addition, hedonic relevance may increase "halo effects" in the sense that many effects come to be grouped together evaluatively. If you offend me, a past action which I thought then to be a gesture of good will may now be reinterpreted as ingratiation. Jones and Davis suggest that relevance increases correspondence, and that since we react more strongly to correspondent inferences, we will in turn evaluate the other more positively or negatively when his behavior has hedonic relevance for us.

The final variable, suggested by Jones and Davis as influential in increasing correspondence and the extremity of evaluation responses, is *personalism*, which is a special class of Heider's category of perceived personal causality. Personal causality implies that the other person intended to produce the effects; personalism implies that the presence or the attributes of the perceiver contributed to the actor's intent to produce the effects. I perceive your actions as having been at least partially influenced by my presence. In essence, I perceive your behavior as directed toward me and as attempting to influence my state. Personalism also represents a special case or intensification of the factors discussed under hedonic relevance. Surely, if another's actions and their effects are directed particularly toward the perceiver himself, the implications of those effects will be stronger.

The attribution of intentions and personality characteristics or dispositions to others results, then, from a complex processing of information regarding qualities of the environment and of the person. The actual process of such attribution is surely not so conscious and rationalistic as Heider and Jones and Davis imply, but their models will serve as working descriptions of the processes of perceiving others. In the next section we will examine the evidence related to these propositions in order to determine how adequately they describe attribution processes.

RELEVANT LITERATURE

While a great amount of research literature relevant to the general attribution process exists, we will consider only studies which bear most directly on the original Heider model and the modifications by Jones and Davis. The research literature will be grouped into four classes: perceptions of internal and external causality, perceptions of *can* and *try*, attributions of responsibility, and inferences about real attitudes from expressed attitudes.

Attribution of Causality

The earliest social psychological experiment using Heider's ideas on causality was conducted by Thibaut and Riecken (1955). They were interested in the relationship between feelings for another and his compliance. They reasoned that a person who complies to a request may do so either because he wants to from feelings of good will (internal causality) or because he feels constrained to comply in the face of threats or promises (external causality). They reasoned further that if a person of relatively high power complies, he will most likely be perceived as having complied because he wanted to, but the low-power person's compliance will be more likely to be attributed to external forces. This prediction makes a certain amount of intuitive sense when we realize that high-power people have a larger range of outcomes under their control (Thibaut and Kelley, 1959) and, hence, greater freedom.

Thibaut and Riecken ran two experiments in which the subject asked both a high- and a low-status confederate to comply with a reasonable request and both complied. Although the data do not permit unequivocal interpretation (partly because the confederates were not equally good at their roles), in general, the locus of causality was seen as internal for the high-status confederates, and as external for the low-status compliers. They also found that the high-status compliers were liked better than the low-status compliers. There was more correspondence between behavior and attributed intent for the high-status confederates; they were perceived as acting primarily from feelings of good will rather than from external pressures.

Consider another type of situation. When a person changes his behavior dramatically, a perceiver might be interested in whether he changed because some dispositional property not manifested earlier had been aroused or because he was forced to change. One key determinant of the attribution would certainly be the salience of any external forces. Hastorf *et al.* (1965) reasoned that the person who changes his behavior in the presence of strong external pressures will be seen as less responsible for the changes than will someone who changes in the presence of weak external pressures, and hence the evaluation of the former will change less. Previous research (Bavelas *et al.*, 1965) had shown that in small discussion groups, the group structure could be changed by the systematic application of reinforcement techniques. Specifically, subjects who talked little in an initial discussion were given nonpublic reinforcements for talking more in a second discussion. Not only did they talk considerably more in the second discussion session, but the ratings of their leadership and quality of ideas given them by the other group members also increased. If the other group members perceived those subjects' increased verbal output as due to internal causality (e.g., "He really is a good talker; he just needed the first discussion to get warmed up."), the higher leadership and ideas ratings make sense. The Hastorf *et al.* (1965) study was designed to test this interpretation. Subjects listened to tape recordings of two discussion sessions in which the lowest talker in the first became the highest talker in the second. The control subjects merely listened to the tapes, whereas the experimental subjects were informed in addition each time a participant had received a reinforcement for talking. As predicted, when asked to rate the participants, the latter saw the increased talker as acting under the influence of external forces, and they were less likely to see his leadership capacity as changing upward.

Moving beyond the Thibaut and Riecken and the Hastorf *et al.* results, we suggest that perceptions of external causality are a direct function of the perceived strength or salience of environmental forces and an inverse function of the perceived power of the individual to withstand environmental forces. This perceptual tendency does not always reflect the true state of affairs. The mere fact that a higher-status person is perceived to have greater ability to withstand enviromental pressures does not imply that he will resist them; he may not try to resist. Similarly, the fact that environmental pressures are perceived to increase does not mean that such pressures are necessarily more responsible for behavior. People may have the capacity to withstand environmental pressures, and furthermore, such pressures operate in many situations to produce behavior the individual wanted to perform anyway. For example, a man may decide to go to the movies; if his wife then suggests that they go to a movie, his behavior is not produced by the wife's request, yet it may well be perceived that way. Part of a four-year-old's willful independence or the "Please, mother, I'd rather do it myself" syndrome surely stems from desires to appear (to both self and others) independent of external forces

If the proposition is correct that perceived external causality is a function of the apparent power of external forces and of apparent internal "strength", then lower-status people should be seen in general as more subject to environmental forces than higher-status people, and the attribution should become more correspondent the more powerful or salient the environmental force. This situation has great implications for the social psychology of supervisor-subordinate relations since, among other things, the supervisor may try to get conformity to his standards through the application of reward and punishment, forces which are external to the subordinate person.

Strickland (1958) tested the proposition that monitoring of subordinates would bias the attribution process. Each subject acted as a supervisor of two workers who performed a boring task for 10 trials. The subject was asked to monitor the performance of worker *A* on 9 trials and of *B* on only 2 trials, and he could fine each worker for failing to perform up to a standard. In reality the persons being supervised were not workers, but the subject was not aware of that fact since he was provided with realistic records of performance. Despite the fact that *A* and *B* had nearly identical and acceptable performances, the subject-supervisor indicated on a questionnaire that he trusted *B* more than *A* and that he saw *A*'s performance as more externally controlled than *B*'s. The hedonic relevance of the workers' behavior was high, and since the subject-supervisors saw their monitoring pressure as high, the behavior of *A*, who was monitored more often, was seen as externally caused.

An experiment by Johnson, Feigenbaum, and Weibey (1964) points to an autistic factor in similar situations. Teachers were asked to rate two children: *A*, who always performed well; and *B*, who performed consistently poorly for some teachers and improved dramatically for others. The teachers attributed the consistently poor performance of *B* to factors internal to the child (poor ability and motivation) and attributed the improvement of *B* to their own (the teachers') efforts, although they also saw the improving *B* as having higher skills and motivation than the nonimproving *B*. Teachers of the improving student seemed to see their own teaching as better than did teachers of the consistently poor student (certainly a realistic perception). It may be argued that, at least from the teacher's perspective, effective teaching operates as a more dramatic influence than does ineffective teaching. If good teaching is perceived as a stronger environmental force than bad teaching, then the fact that the improvement of a student is perceived as due to forces external to him fits our hypothesis that strong external forces bias the attribution process toward an inference of external causality. Note that we can use the word "bias" because the teacher may have taken credit for improvement which was due entirely to the student's own dispositions. We are prone to alter our perception of causality so as to protect or enhance our self-esteem. We attribute success to our own dispositions and failure to external forces, usually unkind or unfair.

Streufert and Streufert (1969) obtained results similar to those of Johnson *et al.* When subjects were successful at a task they saw their success as internally caused. They were less prone to see failure as internally caused. Kite (1964) also found that when workers performed a task successfully, supervisors attributed behavior to the supervisory techniques of reward or punishment (i.e., the behavior was externally caused) more than when the workers failed. In a poor performance situation, when the supervisor had used punishment (which was perceived as a stronger external force than reward), the subject's behavior was perceived as less internally caused than when the supervisor had used reward. Again, the perception of a strong environmental force biases attribution toward external causality.

Some support for the notion that involvement (hedonic relevance and personalism) of the perceiver in the situation biases the attribution of causality comes from experiments by Polefka (1965) and Gross (1966). In both studies subjects tried to change the attitudes of another and either succeeded or did not. Those studies bear considerable resemblance to the work situation if we can assume that attitude change is equivalent to high performance. There was a tendency for the subjects to see their own arguments as better than observers saw the same arguments. Both Polefka and Gross had predicted that subjects would show a greater tendency to perceive attitude change as caused by their own arguments (i.e., external forces) than would observers because the subjects' own hedonic relevance and personalism were higher. In spite of some ambiguities in the data, both sets of results tend in the predicted direction. More research should be directed to the effects of hedonic relevance and personalism on attribution of causality.

There are at least two points about the literature just reviewed which are worth attention. The first concerns the possible asymmetry between compliance and noncompliance in producing attribution of causality. For example, Thibaut and Riecken (1955) showed that the compliance of a high-status other is seen as more internally caused than that of the low-status complier. The reader may wish to speculate about what attributions would have resulted from noncompliance by the two kinds of stimulus persons. Our own speculation is that the compliance pressure would be perceived as too weak to get compliance from the high-status target, but that the non-compliance of the low-status person would be attributed to internal factors—obstinacy, bad intentions.

A second, related question concerns the special role of the perceiver who attempts to get compliance. Compliance pressures which are produced by the perceiver (i.e., are internal to him) are external to the other. Under these circumstances it is not surprising that the perceiver attributes his failure to obtain compliance to the internal dispositions of the other. Such attributions help preserve the perceiver's feeling that his compliance pressures were powerful and legitimate. It must be suggested, then, that attributions to the other in these situations are a bit suspect, inasmuch as both the perceptual stabilities and the ego of the perceiver are strengthened by such attributions.

When we say that a person's behavior was internally caused we are saying that he behaved as he did because he wanted to, because his dispositional qualities were such that he could and wanted to perform that behavior. In this sense, perceptions of internal causality and explanations in terms of intentionality are prerequisite for and almost synonymous with high correspondence of attribution. The act stemmed from stable internal qualities.

We have argued that the stability of our perceptions of others is enhanced by such internal attribution. When we feel we know why a person did one thing, we feel we can predict his behavior in other situations. In the most general of attributions, we may come to feel that well-intentioned people do good acts, and even if we are overwhelmed with a bad act by such a person, we can perceive the bad act as having been externally caused; the person didn't mean to do it. It is interesting to note that the Japanese language actually contains a grammatical form (the passive causative) which permits the speaker to communicate that his behavior was caused by someone else. The form can be used as a way of excusing oneself (Fukuda, 1969).

The tendency to discount information discrepant with our expectations may operate so powerfully that the behavior of the "good" person is interpreted to accord with his perceived intentions. Hastorf and Cantril (1954) demonstrated this outcome by comparing the perceptions of Dartmouth and Princeton students when they were shown a movie of a football game between the two schools that had been judged both rough and dirty by the press. The two groups of students differed markedly in the number of infractions they saw on the part of their own team as compared with the opposing team. Their own team was seen as less rough and dirty. Countless short stories and novels are built around discoveries that the community banker has embezzled money, that the kindly minister has a shady past, or that a well-known gangster loves small children or gives anonymously to charity. The dramatic impact of such stories attests to the extent of our "good people do good acts and bad people do bad acts" attribution.

Ability and Trying

Typically, failure or lack of response to some request creates a greater attribution problem than does success or compliance. That this should occur follows from the earlier analysis in which we pointed out that success gives evidence that the person can do some required behavior and that he has exerted some effort. When he fails, however, it may not be immediately obvious whether the quality he lacks is ability or motivation. For a teacher, for a supervisor, and for a parent the reasons for failure are important. Has too hard a task been set? Are the workers not being paid enough? Despite the theoretical and practical importance of this topic, far too little research has been directed toward it.

Kite (1964) and Rothbart (1968) investigated attributions of trying in a supervisory situation in which a worker clearly could do the task; it involved crossing out certain letters in rows of random letters. Kite assigned some subject-supervisors to use reward and others to use punishment to improve a worker's performance and found that people usually see punishment as a more powerful external motivating force than reward. When the performance did not improve, the punishing supervisors were more likely than the rewarding supervisors to see the workers as not trying. A worker's nonresponsiveness to the perceived stronger external force was seen as evidence of his lack of motivation or interest. It could be argued, however, that subject-supervisors would have had different reactions if they had freely chosen to use either reward or punishment. Rothbart investigated this question. His principal interest lay in determining factors which affect choice of reward or punishment, and he found that highly motivated supervisors used less punishment and more reward than did the less highly motivated supervisors. The highly motivated subject-supervisors (who used reward, the weaker external force) were less inclined to attribute failure to lack of trying than were the supervisors who used punishment.

There have been even fewer studies on ability attribution, but one by E. E. Jones *et al.* (1968), which raises a number of important issues about ability attribution, will be discussed in some detail. In five related experiments, subjects observed a stimulus person perform a series of 30 intelligence-test-type items of considerable difficulty. Although there were a variety of conditions, in the three of interest to us the stimulus person (1) started out well and then declined in performance (descend), or (2) started out poorly and improved (ascend), or (3) performed consistently throughout (random). In each case the stimulus person answered 15 of 30 items correctly. Then on a second series of 30 items, the stimulus person gave her answers and the subject tried to predict whether they were correct or not. The subject also rated the stimulus person on intelligence and estimated how many correct answers the stimulus person had given on the first set of 30 trials (in effect, a measure of recall). The data are relatively consistent. Descending stimulus persons are seen as more intelligent than either ascending or random-performance stimulus persons, subjects recall descenders as performing better than either ascending or random stimulus persons, and they make more predictions of success in the descending than in the ascending or random conditions. We can summarize these results by suggesting that subjects attribute more ability to the descending performer than to the ascending or consistent performer, whether the attributions involve predictions of future performance, recall of past performance, or the dispositional property of intelligence.

One explanation for the Jones *et al.* results is that ability is a fundamental dispositional property and it is quite stable over time. Once having attributed an ability to a person, we must find other explanations for failure other than lack of ability, e.g., lack of motivation or disinterest. The descending stimulus person has ability attributed to him early (remember our earlier reasoning that success implies ability), and the subjects may see future performance as due to "try" variables (although, unfortunately, such a possibility was not directly checked out in this experiment). The ascending performers are just beginning to give evidence of their ability at the end of the series, and it can easily be shown that until the last item the descending stimulus person has done better than the ascending; in other words, the descending stimulus person has given more evidence of ability than has the ascending stimulus person throughout the series prior to answering the final item. The person who starts out strong may appear to be intelligent and bored with the routine nature of the task, while the ascending subject may be seen to have a less quick mind. In a comparison with the parable of the hare and the tortoise, we may identify the ascender with the tortoise—a bit slow to catch on but getting there reliably; the descender is the hare—long on ability but short on motivation.

Although Jones *et al.* discuss other explanations for their results, the above interpretation seems most plausible. However, it raises the whole issue of whether ability is "more dispositional" than motivation. Apparently ability is subject to primacy effects and remains quite constant under behavior changes. It does seem likely that most people consider ability to be more dispositional than motivation. After all, ability is invariant over a wide variety of tasks and situations, whereas each of us knows that motivation changes with time and the situation.

Attributions of ability and motivation have important consequences. You may well imagine that a teacher reacts quite differently to a student who fails because he is "in over his head" than to one who fails because he is "lazy." The classic experiments directed to this problem were conducted by Jones and deCharms (1957). In an initial experiment they suggested that if another's failure had consequences for the subject (high hedonic relevance), he would be evaluated less positively than he would be if hedonic relevance was low. The manipulation of consequences was simple. Several subjects worked on intellectual tasks and one subject (actually a confederate) failed. In the high-consequence condition an individual's failure meant that the whole group failed, whereas in the low-consequence condition only the confederate failed. There was some support for the hypothesis that the failing confederate would be more negatively evaluated in the high-consequence condition than in the individual-failure condition. In the former the confederate was also seen as less dependable.

One plausible reason for the weak results obtained in this experiment was that failing people are not held accountable for lack of ability in the same way they are for lack of motivation. The experimenters had emphasized that failure would be due to lack of ability. A second experiment was then conducted in which consequences were again manipulated; this time it was strongly implied to the subjects that failure could be due either to poor ability or to lack of motivation. Although the results were again equivocal, there was a greater tendency in the high-consequence than in any other condition to evaluate lower the confederate who failed for motivational reasons. He was also seen as particularly low in dependability. The results of the two experiments taken together suggest that people are held responsible for failures that have consequences for others, particularly when the failure resulted from not trying.

There are a number of experiments which bear on that general hypothesis. For example, Lanzetta and Hannah (1969) showed that supervisors gave stronger punishments to high-ability than to lower-ability subjects who fail. That result was particularly marked when the task was difficult. One interpretation of the result is that when failure is less attributable to lack of ability and more to lack of trying, supervisors will be more likely to hold the learner responsible for his failure and to punish him out of frustration. A variety of other experiments have shown that when a subject perceives his frustration as arbitrary or caused by the motivational or personality problems of another, he reacts to it more negatively than to similar frustration which can't be helped (Schmitt, 1964; Pastore, 1952; Berkowitz, 1962; Burnstein and Worchel, 1962).

It seems reasonable that people are held responsible for a lack of trying, primarily because not trying seems to imply bad intentions. By not trying to help another, the person indicates his dislike for or some bad intention toward the other. There is other evidence (Pepitone and Sherberg, 1957) that subjects who are perceived as having bad intentions are considered particularly responsible for failure.

The research literature seems to point to two general conclusions. First, abilities are seen as more dispositional, and more invariant, than is motivation. The second is that failure resulting from lack of motivation is thought to be more reprehensible than failure due to lack of ability. Let us now consider these propositions in the broader context of assignment of responsibility.

Attribution of Responsibility

People are held responsible for the effects of their behavior on some occasions but not on others. Heider (1958) suggested that people are held responsible only for effects they intended to create and, by implication, effects they have the ability to create. In short, people are held responsible only for acts and their effects which result from personal causation and not for those resulting from impersonal causation. Heider believed further that the tendency to assign responsibility in this manner should show changes during the development of the individual. Given Piaget's discoveries that young children overattribute causality, Heider hypothesized that younger children would see another as responsible for effects connected with him in any way (*A* is responsible if *B* hits a pedestrian with *A*'s car). A second developmental stage would be distinguishable by assignment of responsibility only for effects resulting from the action of the stimulus person (*A* is responsible for hitting a pedestrian with his car even if the pedestrian suddenly walked out in front of him). In the third stage, the person would be held responsible only for the effects he could foresee (*A* is responsible for hitting a pedestrian if he was not carefully watching for someone to walk out in front of him). In the fourth stage, the person would be considered responsible only for intended effects. (*A* is responsible only if he intended to hit a pedestrian.) In the fifth developmental stage, he would not be held entirely responsible even for acts that he intended. (*A* is not responsible for hitting the pedestrian, even though he intended to, because his nagging mother-in-law in the back seat provoked him to do it.)

Support for these developmental stages of responsibility assignment has been obtained in studies by Shaw and Sulzer (1964), Shaw (1967), and Sulzer and Burglass (1968). They present evidence that in assigning responsibility, adults take intentions into account more than children do. One interesting and unanticipated result of the Shaw and Sulzer research was the subjects' tendencies to attribute more responsibility to an actor whose actions resulted in negative rather than positive outcomes, especially when the outcomes were intense. Walster (1966) also investigated the effects of the nature of the outcome on the assignment of responsibility. She had each of her subjects hear one of four tape recordings about a young man whose automobile accidentally rolled down a hill. The results of the accident were the varying conditions reported on the tapes. Either a small or a large amount of damage was done to the car itself, or in its descent the car either came close to hitting a man and child or actually did hit them. Thus Walster varied the factors of both severity of outcome and injury to someone besides the main character. The data show that the young man was held more responsible when the outcome was severe and especially when it involved other people. If we can assume that severe negative outcomes have greater impact on perceivers than mild outcomes, these findings can be interpreted as supporting the Jones and Davis (1965) hypothesis that hedonic relevance increases correspondence; in this instance, it increases strength of responsibility attribution. It appears that the perceiver has an increasing need to attribute responsibility to someone as the outcomes become more severe.

These research results seem to support several general propositions. (1) Behavior is seen as internally caused when external forces are not very powerful and/or when ability to withstand external forces is high. (2) Internal forces are seen as instances of personal causality to the extent that the person has high ability and high motivation. (3) Ability is perceived as more dispositional than is trying, but whether or not a person is perceived as intending the effects of an act is a significant determiner of praise and blame. (4) The tendencies toward the perceptions proposed above increase when the effects of behavior have high hedonic relevance.

Attribution of Attitude

It is obvious that in social life people may on occasion make statements they do not believe. People may publicly conform to the group's attitudes for a variety of reasons (Kiesler and Kiesler, 1969), and there is always the possibility that a person may lie in order to ingratiate (Jones, 1964). Needless to say, there are also more benign forms of distortion. Gouldner (1960), Goffman (1955), and others have pointed to powerful norms in our society which tend to guarantee that in specified circumstances certain kinds of information will be communicated. A friend who has failed an exam is usually comforted; the "faces," or self-presentations, of others are usually accepted in public. Furthermore, we tend to tailor our public pronouncements to fit the existing attitudes of our audiences, at least in "polite company"; too much disagreement is in bad taste. Under these circumstances, we may find inferring the real attitudes and beliefs of another problematical. Given that there are occasions when there is no correspondence between another's true attitudes and his public behavior, we have an attribution problem. The public behavior could be a function of internal factors (real attitudes) or external factors (normative demands).

The Jones and Davis (1965) attribution model provides a useful analysis of this problem. Implicit in the analysis is the assumption that behavior is a conscious decision in the light of alternative courses of action. Let us examine for a moment our perceptions of a politician's "true" attitudes. In running for office, a politician must balance off several competing pressures. He may want to state his own opinion on various issues, but he must also take care that his public expression on them is popular enough with the electorate and sufficiently congruent with his party's policy to gain election. The extent to which a politician's stated opinion on an issue is popular with the public and/or *in-role* (congruent with his party's policy) affects the perception of that opinion as an expression of his true beliefs. In the 1968 presidential election many people felt unclear about Vice President Humphrey's real stand on Vietnam since he chose to support administration policy in general. His behavior was in-role, and consequently, attribution of real attitude became difficult.

We feel confident that a man states his own beliefs when he moves out-of-role and goes against public opinion; role and social-approval forces are thought to be so strong that we ascribe great courage to men who state their convictions in the face of such demands to the contrary. The point is, then, that unpopular and out-of-role behaviors require so much courage that we are quite confident that a person who performs such behavior is speaking his own mind. The attribution of true attitude is then very easy. Evidence from experiments by Jones *et al.* (1961) and Steiner and Field (1960) support the general position that behavior out-of-role leads to more correspondent (i.e., more extreme and more confident) attributions.

An experiment designed to test those ideas was conducted by Jones and Harris (1967). Their basic reasoning was that a subject will be most able to make a correspondent attribution of true attitude to a person who states an unpopular position and does so by choice. That much had been shown by Steiner and Field (1960). To test the model it was desirable not only to replicate their findings but also to show what results would obtain when the stimulus person took a popular position. Theoretically, then, the public attitude stated by a person who has no choice about which attitude to state is not informative about that person's real attitude, but the same behavior under conditions of choice does say something about his real attitude. Figure 4.2 gives the theoretical predictions and general results obtained in three experiments.

	Attitude attribution	
	Theoretical prediction	*Result*
Pro-popular position (choice)	Highly pro	Highly pro
Pro-popular position (no choice)	Moderately pro	Moderately pro (with great variability of attribution)
Anti-popular position (choice)	Extremely anti	Extremely anti
Anti-popular position (no choice)	Moderately pro	Moderately anti

Figure 4.2

The results in general support the model, with one exception. The people who have no choice and take an unpopular position are perceived to hold that unpopular position at least moderately strongly. The model predicts that perceivers should have no information about the subjects' real views, and yet they seem to feel they do. This result may be a function of what Heider (1958) suggested was the tendency of "behavior to engulf the field" and assume too great a weight in attribution. Perhaps we really do judge people more on their behavior than on their intentions. An alternative explanation of that finding is also possible. The subjects in the Jones and Harris experiment who argued unpopular positions did a good job of arguing. Perhaps the cogency of their arguments was "held against" them. They were required only to argue the position; their eloquence was apparently taken as evidence of conviction. People who are forced to argue against their own positions ought to do so with minimal persuasiveness.

There is some evidence from one of the Jones and Harris experiments which bears on the latter interpretation. In that experiment subjects were instructed to give a speech either in favor of or against a popular position, and each gave an ambiguous speech. The very ambivalence of the speech indicated that the subject's heart was not in what he was doing under instruction. Thus the inference that the subject really believed the opposite of what he was instructed to say was facilitated. The data support this conjecture. When the speech itself was ambivalent, subjects instructed to give the pro-speech were seen as more anti than subjects who were instructed to give the anti-speech. Jones and Harris have shown that when situational forces are strong, a person's behavior is relatively uninformative about his true attitudes. When external forces are low, greater correspondence is perceived and perceivers are likely to see the person as sincere. Jones and Harris employed choice/no choice as their manipulation of environmental pressures; normative pressure is a much more pervasive environmental force.

If no environmental normative forces can be seen to exist, then the person's public behavior is usually seen as a reflection of his true attitudes. If a speaker gives a speech likely to be well received by his audience, we might attribute his action either to his desire to make a good impression or to his real opinions. At the same time, if he gives the same speech to an audience which will not like its content, the principal attribution would be that he has spoken his true beliefs. This argument is quite analogous to the arguments presented by Jones and Davis (1965) on out-of-role attributions. Mills and Jellison (1967) found that a speech given to a "hostile" audience was perceived as more sincere than the same speech given to a "friendly" audience. Furthermore, subjects in the former audience were more persuaded.

Eisinger and Mills (1968) extended this thinking in an experiment concerned with the effects of extremity on perceived sincerity. They found that subjects perceived a communicator who argued an extreme position on either side of an issue as more sincere than a communicator who argued a moderate position. If the communicator argues the subject's own position, it is plausible that the sincerity may be merely a function of agreement with the subject. On the other hand, if the communicator takes an extreme position counter to that of the subject, perceived sincerity may be due to the perception that he has taken an unpopular position. Eisinger and Mills present evidence for the correctness of these explanations. Thus the perception of sincerity seems to be a function of the person's capacity to counteract normative, external forces. Interestingly enough, Eisinger and Mills also found that perceived competence is an inverse linear function of discrepancy between own and communicator's positions; the extreme communicator on the other side may be perceived as sincere, but he is also seen as incompetent. It appears that ability and motivational factors are attributed quite differently in that situation.

The research of Mills and his colleagues demonstrates that people will question the sincerity of an expressed attitude when there are strong normative pressures for such expression. Attitudes are perceived as more sincere when they are expressed against normative pressures. Clearly, the same doubts could be entertained about expressed compliments. The normative pressures for saying nice things to another are very great. Since approval is typically more normative than criticism, people should see criticism as more sincere and candid. That result was found by Dickoff (1961) and by Landy and Aronson (1968). Schneider (1965) demonstrated that an evaluator who gave negative as well as positive evaluations was judged as more candid than the uniformly positive evaluator. Thus approval, like attitudes, seems to be assessed in light of its relationship to normative demands.

Earlier in this chapter we suggested that strong external forces bias the attribution process in favor of seeing those forces as responsible for the behavior. In this section we have gone one step further. If indeed most people respond to strong external forces—in this case normative pressures—then attribution to internal factors (real attitude, candor, etc.) is facilitated when people are seen as resisting such forces. This interpretation is consistent with Jones and Davis' argument that correspondence is facilitated when the behavior is socially undesirable.

SELF-ATTRIBUTION

It may have occurred to the reader that many of the attribution processes discussed thus far might also be applied to the attribution of qualities to one's self. It could be argued that people are motivated to explain their own behavior in terms of environmental forces and self forces. In principle, the process of self-attribution need not differ from attribution to others. Kelley's (1967) analysis of attribution stresses the continuities between self- and other-attribution.

There are two general inferential models of self-attribution, both of which are consistent in many respects with the work we have already reviewed, provided that one is willing to assume that self-attribution is a process similar to other-attribution. The first model, which was proposed by Bem (1967), emphasizes inferences which are made on the basis of observing one's own behavior, and the second (Schachter, 1964; Valins, 1966) is chiefly concerned with the relationship between perception of the situation and emotional labeling.

The Bem analysis was originally conceived as an alternative to the theory of cognitive dissonance (Festinger, 1957). Before outlining Bem's theory, we will review some key dissonance experiments in order to provide a context for the following discussion. In the initial statement of the theory, Festinger defined dissonance as a function of the number, the relevance, and the importance of contradictory cognitions. Dissonance is assumed to be uncomfortable, and the individual is therefore motivated to reduce it, usually by altering his cognitions about either the world or himself. When a person says one thing and believes another, dissonance is created. Since the cognition about what one has said cannot easily be changed, dissonance in this case will most likely be reduced by bringing one's belief more in line with the statement. However, to the extent that the person had justification for engaging in the behavior, the dissonance is lessened; another cognition, consonant with the cognition that one has made the statement, has been added. The "lie" is justified.

The classic experiment in this area was conducted by Festinger and Carlsmith (1959). Subjects worked on a boring task and were then recruited to tell another subject that the task had been interesting. They were offered either $1 or $20 for the "lie," and to the extent that the payment justified the act, dissonance was expected to be lessened. The prediction then was that subjects would experience more dissonance and would change their attitudes more about how interesting the task was in the $1 condition. The prediction was confirmed. Subjects saw the task as more interesting when they had been paid the smaller amount of money for telling another person it was interesting. When subjects engaged in counterattitudinal behavior, they change their attitudes toward their public behavior to the extent that there is inadequate justification. Festinger and Carlsmith's results have been replicated many times in a variety of experimental situations (cf. Zimbardo and Ebbesen, 1969).

Bem's explanation for these results begins with the question of what a naive observer would predict the subject's private opinion to be if he knew only (1) what the subject had said and (2) how much the subject had been paid for making the statement. The observer could attribute the publicly stated attitude to internal causes ("that's his real attitude") or to external causes ("he's only doing it for the money"). To the extent that perceivers operate in an either/or fashion, namely, that one or the other cause is the only cause, they will be led to conclude that the highly paid subject probably performed the action for the money, the poorly paid subject because he really believed it. The reasoning might be something like the following: If the subject made the speech for as little as $1, he must surely believe what he said since $1 is not a very powerful incentive for him to lie about his beliefs. If he made the speech for $20, then he may well have been lying since most people would probably tell a small lie for such a large amount of money. Thus the perceiver might be inclined to attribute the subject's speech to his real attitudes when external forces are not very strong ($1) and to external forces when they are ($20). We could also relate this analysis to our discussion in the last section of the role of perceived external forces in the attribution process.

Bem does show (1965, 1967) that subjects exposed to the instructions of the Festinger and Carlsmith experiment and to information about the subject's speech and payment did infer that the $20 subject enjoyed the experiment less than the $1 subject did. In other words, perceivers seem to see subjects' behavior as more under the influence of external forces that are perceived to be strong.

Bem argues that the Festinger-Carlsmith subjects acted like outside observers in assessing their own attitudes. Perhaps the subjects in the original Festinger and Carlsmith experiment changed their attitudes through some similar attribution process. We might assume that initially the subjects did not have particularly clear attitudes about how interesting the task had been, but that when asked by the experimenter to indicate their attitudes, they relied on perceptions of their own behavior. The $20 subjects may have said to themselves, "I guess the task was boring since I was paid so much money for saying it was interesting." The $1 subjects may have said "I guess the task was interesting since I said it was interesting for such a small amount of money. The only real justification Icould have had for saying so is that it's true." So the $1 subjects may simply have attributed greater internal causality to themselves than the $20 subjects did.

There is one major problem with the epistemological status of Bem's analysis. Bem shows only that observers of a subject's behavior *can* produce results which are highly similar to the subject's real responses. This does not, of course, mean that the subjects *do* act as observers of their own behavior although there is certainly a reasonable possibility that they do. Logically, one cannot conclude that Bem has shown that his explanation is the best one for dissonance experiments, but only that it is a possible and reasonable one, a point which Bem (1968) readily concedes.

There is an additional methodological problem with Bem's analysis of forced-compliance experiments. Bem's observers were not given information about whether or not all subjects in the initial dissonance experiment complied with the request to make the counterattitudinal statement. Virtually all subjects in those experiments did agree to make the statement, but if the Bem observers did not realize that fact, they may have decided that there was subject self-selection. That is, the attribution of a more favorable attitude to the $1 subjects may reflect the feeling that to do the job for $1, a subject must have been initially favorable to the topic. In other words, any subject who did not agree would have refused to make the statement for such a small amount of money. That criticism was made by Kelley (1967) and by R. A. Jones *et al.* (1968). The latter authors showed in a number of experiments that when subjects' initial attitudes are made salient for observers, the observers do not replicate the usual result (more favorable attitudes for less payment). Bem's (1968) reply to the Jones *et al.* criticism is also a reasonable one. He points out that the issue really hinges on the extent to which subjects are aware of their own initial attitudes. If a subject's initial attitudes are salient, then he has more information about his own cognitive state than the observer has. If the initial attitudes are not salient, then the subject and the observer are probably in analogous positions. The key experimental question seems to be to what extent the subjects' own initial attitudes in the dissonance experiments were salient.

Although there have been other attempts (Kiesler *et al.*, 1969) to test dissonance theory versus Bemian explanations experimentally, more central for our concerns are attempts to extend Bem's analysis to other areas of self-perception. In one such experiment, Bandler *et al.* (1968) investigated the experience of pain. If a subject chose to escape from shock, an observer might reason that the shock must have been painful; if the subject did not choose to escape, then the observer might infer that the shock could not have been very painful. In fact, subjects who were encouraged to escape the shocks after they were turned on reported them as more painful than did the subjects who had not escaped them. This is really an example of attribution to environmental forces. The shocks (i.e., external forces) must have been powerful since the subjects tried to escape them.

Bem's subject-as-observer model will undoubtedly stimulate needed research on the processes of self-attribution. As yet, however, not enough data have been collected to assess the model's limitations and generality.

Another line of research on the question of self-attribution has been concerned with labeling of emotional states. Schachter (1964; Schachter and Wheeler, 1962; Schachter and Singer, 1962; Nisbett and Schachter, 1966) has emphasized the role of the stimulus situation in defining emotion. In an earlier day William James (1890) suggested that our labeling of emotions involves our perceptions of our own behavior, and subsequent evidence has encouraged the belief that external events partially define felt emotion. According to Schachter's theory, arousal is a necessary condition for the perception of one's own emotional state, but the particular emotion the person "feels" will be determined by environmental cues. Schachter and Singer (1962) aroused subjects by injecting them with epinephrine (adrenalin). Some subjects were told correctly that the injection was a stimulant, others were told incorrectly that it was a depressant, and a third group were given no information. Then the subjects were exposed to a happy confederate or an aggressive one. The injection produced bodily arousal, and the two confederates provided different possible situational definitions. In general, those subjects who had not been given by the experimenter an adequate explanation for their arousal (i.e., the no-information and misinformed conditions) reported emotions more congruent with the confederate's behavior, and they also behaved more emotionally. It is likely that persons who experience arousal with no clear prior explanation for it will look to the environment for their labels.

Nisbett and Schachter (1966) extended these results to the perception of pain. Subjects were given a placebo, and half of them were told the drug would cause the same symptoms that strong shock would cause; the other half were told nothing. Subjects were then given strong shock. The subjects who could attribute the shock-related symptoms to the drug reported less pain than did the other subjects. The result suggests that the labeling of experiences of pain is in part controlled by available situational cues.

The research by Schachter and his students seems to indicate that when a subject is in a state of unclear emotional arousal, strong environmental forces (the behavior of a confederate, the expectation of a drug's effects) tend to bias the attribution processes toward external definition. In a sense, the subject experiences the feeling which powerful external forces say he should.

Further information on attribution to the environment comes from a research program carried out by Valins and his colleagues. Valins (1966) conducted an experiment investigating the extent to which internal stimuli are used to label feelings. He reasoned that emotional experiences of subjects should be influenced by the perception of internal stimuli. He provided subjects with amplified feedback of "your heartbeat" (the feedback was actually preprogrammed) while they looked at *Playboy* centerfolds. During exposure to half the pictures the heartrate remained constant for all subjects and to the other half increased for some subjects, decreased for the others. As Valins had hypothesized, the subjects rated the pictures as more attractive when their heartrate had changed (either increased or decreased), presumably because they had had evidence of greater emotional arousal in those conditions. The pictures that had been accompanied by changed heartrate were also preferred as payment for the experiment.

Later Valins extended his research to include the perception of fear. Valins and Ray (1967) chose subjects who were afraid of snakes. Snakes were the feared stimulus; shock was used as a control stimulus. Some subjects heard their "heartrate" increase to the shock stimulus but not to pictures of snakes. A control group that also received shock and saw snake pictures were given no information about internal reactions. As predicted, the control subjects had a greater fear of snakes in a behavioral test than the experimental subjects did. The latter had evidence that they were aroused by shock but not by snakes. Therefore, presumably, they could not be afraid of snakes.

Davison and Valins (1969) raised the further question whether self-attribution in such situations can play a role in the maintenance of behavior change. Subjects whose behavior changes in conjunction with drug therapy (e.g., tranquilizers) can easily attribute such changes to the drug as an external force and do not interpret them as changes in their own personalities. If behavior change is to be maintained after drugs are withdrawn, it is necessary to convince the subject that a "real" (i.e., self-induced) change has occurred. In their experiment, Davison and Valins gave subjects a series of painful shocks. They then gave the subjects a "drug" called paratoxin (actually a placebo), and the subjects were told that paratoxin would make shocks less painful to them. After the paratoxin had "taken effect," the subjects were given a second series of shocks. Unknown to the subjects, the second shocks were lower in intensity so that the subjects believed they had tolerated more shock in the second than in the first series. Then half the subjects were told that paratoxin was actually a placebo, and the other half were told that the effects of the paratoxin had "worn off." When a third series of shocks was administered, the researchers found that the group that had been told that paratoxin was a placebo withstood more shock than did the group that believed in the paratoxin's effectiveness. Both groups of subjects thought they had tolerated greater shock in the second than in the first series (remember that the experimenters had cleverly reduced the actual shock intensity without the subjects' knowing it). Although half the subjects could attribute their greater "pain tolerance" to external factors (the "paratoxin"), the other half realized that their greater tolerance could not be due to such external factors (since "paratoxin" had been revealed as a placebo). The latter could attribute their greater tolerance only to internal factors since there were no strong external factors perceived to be at work. It is therefore understandable that they tolerated more shock in the third series because they attributed their tolerance to a dispositional state. Their increased tolerance for pain was attributed to themselves.

At the beginning of this section we stated the assumption that attributions to self and others result from similar processes. It is therefore appropriate to call attention to certain relationships between these two areas of research. Self-attribution is fundamentally a problem in perception of internal-external causality. Earlier we argued that in the perception by one person of another, attribution of external causality is enhanced when (1) external forces are strong and (2) the power of the perceiver to resist external forces is low. The same generalization seems to apply to self-attribution. The research of Bem suggests that the perception of strong external reasons for performing a behavior may lead subjects to see those external forces as causing their behavior. Schachter and Valins have also shown that clear situational cues lead to emotional labeling in terms of those cues. We must point out, however, that the effects in all three areas of research depend on the subjects' having ambiguous, weak, or nonsalient cognitions about their internal states. This, we suggest, is an example of low "internal power." Just as a low-status person is perceived as relatively powerless to resist compliance pressures, so a subject with diffuse rather than articulated emotional arousal is less able to resist situational definitions of his state.

This set of investigations opens up a series of very interesting and important questions that bear on the development of a person's self-concept. The implication is that self-attribution develops out of situations in which the person cannot explain his own behavior by referring to some external force. He can say only "that must have been me" or "that's the kind of person I am." Self-concepts are likely to be most certain when situational forces are weak and unclear. The same dynamics may also have implications for psychotherapeutic processes. Effective therapy or behavior change should require that the change be accompanied by self-attribution because in order for the new behavior to be integrated with the self-concept, it must be perceived as self-caused.

SUMMARY

The attribution process plays, we believe, a significant role in our creation of a stable and sensible social world. Therefore, let us review some of the major propositions we have stated regarding the attribution process. We begin with the phenomenological fact that our perception of others does not stop with the observation of their behavior. We also perceive other people as causal agents or at least as capable of being causal agents. The perception of causality is central in our perception of other people. Put in another way, when Heider talks of our engaging in a naive analysis of action, he means that in our perceptions we go beyond behavior and make causal inferences about why the behavior occurred. When we observe a person's actions, we are impelled to explain why he did what he did. Jones and Davis refer to this process as organizing the behavior of the other person into intent-act-effect units. Our perception of what a person intended is just as important as our knowledge of what he actually did.

We conceive that we begin such an informal analysis by evaluating the apparent strength of environmental or external forces as compared with the strength of internal forces. Then we separate the strength of the internal forces into the components ability (can) and effort (try). When we infer that the combination of ability and effort was stronger than the external forces, we infer that internal causality was present. Only then do we say such things as "he did it because he wanted to" or "she did it because that's the sort of person she is." Note that this is the language of attribution because it includes the assumption that knowledge has been acquired about the other's enduring dispositions. Strong feelings, such as anger, blame, or love, seem to occur only when such dispositional inferences have been made.

We have also stressed that normative pressures and roles are perceived as powerful environmental forces. When they are salient in our perception, we feel that we have gained little knowledge about the other person. We say to ourselves such things as "anyone would have done that" or even "he had to do it." The phenomenon of "in-role" behavior raises some interesting questions concerning how people communicate true positive feeling when positive behavior in general is role-required. How does the physician or the counselor let another person know his positive feelings in such a way that the perceiver doesn't see the message as role-required and forced by external pressures? The phenomenon of attribution to external pressures appears to be very important in self-perception also. When we can attribute our behavior to environmental pressures, we get little feeling of self-knowledge.

It is easy to see how this search for enduring dispositions in others can contribute to the creation of a stable and meaningful social world. Behavior may be ever-changing, but if very different behaviors can be linked to the same intent or disposition, then we have achieved an invariance that provides us with a sensible stability. However, stability does not necessarily imply accuracy. It is possible that we may achieve stability at the cost of accuracy. We shall take up this general question in the next chapter when we explore the relationship between our perceptions of the other person and our behavior toward him.

CHAPTER FIVE

Person Perception and Interpersonal Behavior

In concluding this book, perhaps we should restate our major argument: *The research in person perception has shifted in interest from the stimuli and the accuracy with which they are recorded to the ways that perceivers actively process those stimuli to create interpersonal meaning.* We have argued that such meaning and the demands that we be able to predict the behavior of others require a relatively high degree of stability in our perceptions. We further implied that there are two important kinds of stability. The first is stability of general inference processes. Our implicit personality theories allow us to draw inferences about another based on minimal information, and they appear to be relatively stable since they allow for predictions about various kinds of people. A second kind of stability is attribution stability. We agree with Heider's argument that we need to infer a given other's dispositional properties in order to predict his future behavior.

The two kinds of stability differ in a variety of ways, but we will emphasize their similarities. However, it is fair to stress one difference. Inferential stability primarily concerns stability across people, but attribution stability refers to stability of inferences for a single person over time. We support the hypothesis that attribution stability is the generic process because it serves as the basis of inferential stability; certain traits are inferred to be related because we see them as stemming from the same basic intentions. A way to look at the difference between inferential and attribution stability is to ask what kind of evidence would disrupt each kind of perceptual structure. In the former, disruption would occur if a large number of people were perceived to have a pattern of traits at variance with the implicit personality theory.

If the implicit personality theory suggests that warm people are also honest, then finding a number of warm-dishonest others would tend to reduce the stability of the warm-honest inference. Similarly with attribution stability, disruption occurs if a person exhibits an intent at variance with a previous attribution, e.g., if a friend you have felt to be friendly is now shown to harbor hostile intentions. We stress again that even when behavior is quite variable, stability can be achieved through the attribution of consistent intents. Stability requires that there be little or no contradiction in perceived intentions.

The most obvious point to make about inferential and attribution stability is that stability is maintained to the extent that there are relatively few disconfirmations. Surely we do receive significant disconfirmations, and our cognitive structure must shift in response to them. The fact that we do so raises in turn the question of how perceptions are maintained in a stable state. There seem to be four general reasons why our perceptions are stable, and we will discuss each.

Perceived stability reflects actual stability. The first reason is the most obvious. Perceptual stabilities may result from accurate perceptions of real behavioral and dispositional stabilities. Most perceivers are likely to see warm people as considerate. At the same time, perceivers are likely to judge that a high-status person conformed because he wanted to; such a conclusion may, in fact, correspond to the true state of affairs.

The major problem with this position is that it says both too little and too much. It says too little because it fails to account for obvious cases in which the perceptions are "too" stable. Concern with the halo effect and logical error grew out of the tendency of perceivers to overperceive stability. Racial and national stereotypes are particularly pernicious examples of overstability.

The realist position says too much because it naively assumes that we know what we mean by behavioral and dispositional stability. Conventional trait theory (see Allport, 1937) accounts for behavioral stability in terms of enduring, real traits (e.g., hostility) possessed by the actor. Although evidence in the research literature is mixed, there is some indication that stability of behavior across situations is not high. One can argue that behavioral stability results not from consistency of personality but from consistency of situational pressures (Mischel, 1968). Women may appear to be warmer than men because they are more often in situations (i.e., around children) that elicit warm behavior. Situational cues that elicit hostility may also elicit behavior that could be described as cynical. Thus, if correlations among various kinds of behavior do exist, they could be due to situational invariance rather than dispositional invariance.

Our purpose here is not to take sides between realists, who believe that our perceptions approximate external events, and idealists, who believe that perceivers create their own realities. For example, we would not assert that perceptual stabilities never reflect the behavior of others. It is likely not only that people have enduring personal characteristics but also that they can be perceived accurately. However, we caution the reader to be aware of the likelihood that most, perhaps all perceivers tend to over attribute stability to the behavior of others.

Stability is not absolute. We must also keep in mind that stability is rarely, if ever, absolute. Perceivers do not as a rule make absolute or extreme judgments about another. It would be hard to find a perceiver who would assert that all fat people are jolly, that all warm people are honest, or that a particular friend is completely sincere. In practice this means that exceptions to the general judgments can be tolerated without disconfirming the general rule. A morose fat man and a warm dishonest person are examples of those exceptions which keep the correlations between certain traits less than perfect, and the sincere friend who ingratiates has his lapse attributed to a bad day, an unusual situation, or particularly strong motivation to gain something from us.

We must also point out in this context that subjects in the typical person-perception experiment are asked for more restricted judgments than they may ordinarily make. A common response by subjects asked to rate a friend's kindness is "I can't make such an absolute judgment; it depends on the situation. In some situations he's kind, in others he is not." It is our impression that subjects take situational contingencies into account more than most theorists assume that they do. People also make attributions to the environment. These modifications do not necessarily mean that our emphasis on stability is too strong but only that perceptual stability may be more situation-specific than we have assumed.

Information about others is restricted. Inferences and attributions may be stable because they are practically never disconfirmed. We have already mentioned that one reason our attributions are not disconfirmed is that they may well be accurate. But we must face the fact that they are not always accurate. A third pressure toward the maintenance of stability stems from the nature of interpersonal communications; evidence which might lead to disconfirmation may not be communicated to the perceiver. There are three general reasons for this possible occurrence. In the first place, normative and self-esteem forces inhibit certain kinds of communication. People find it more comfortable to say pleasant than unpleasant things to one another. It is embarrassing to tell another he is wrong. If another perceives me (let us say incorrectly) as particularly intelligent, I may find it ego-enhancing and socially comfortable not to disabuse him of his incorrect perception. I would probably be more likely to try to correct his perception that

I am unkind. Tangential evidence in support of this line of reasoning comes from an experiment by Tagiuri, Blake, and Bruner (1953). They found that subjects in a group knew better who liked them than who disliked them—presumably because indications of liking are communicated more readily than indications of disliking. Furthermore, in certain kinds of situations correcting another's wrong attribution may be particularly difficult. For example, it probably requires more courage and social skill to correct a higher- than a lower-status other, and tact may require that such corrections not be made in public.

Second, interactions are selective. If I know that you perceive me as unintelligent, I would probably be offended and might avoid you, thus denying you the opportunity to correct your impression. If I perceive you as dishonest, I am likely to cease interaction with you, again denying the opportunity for correction. Newcomb (1947) uses the term "autistic hostility" to refer to the latter response, i.e., the tendency to cease interaction with and reduce further information about disliked others. One piece of evidence consistent with this notion comes from Kelley (1950), who found that students who were told their instructors were cold tended to participate in class discussion less than students whose instructors were supposedly warm. By not interacting with the instructors, the former students reduced their chances to find that their instructors were less cold than they had originally thought.

Third, some mistakes in attribution are not disconfirmed because they are unrevealed. Certainly, attributions are often not verbalized, and because adequate conditions for testing them do not exist, they remain implicit. For example, an employer may judge that *A* is more competent than *B* and hire *A*. Even if *B* is actually more competent, the employer suffers no ill consequences from his error of attribution, so long as *A* performs well; he never has a chance to see *B* perform. Similarly, directors of admission in selective colleges may find out that they have incorrectly admitted some students, but they will not usually discover which students they have incorrectly not admitted.

It is easy to assume that perceptions operate according to some feedback principle such that errors tend to correct the perceptions. Undoubtedly this assumption proves valid under at least some contingencies. All we are suggesting is that most social situations bias the feedback. In the language of modern communication theory the signal-to-noise ratio in social communication is quite low. Given the peculiar biases of the social structure, it is relatively harder to get disconfirmation than confirmation for a particular attribution or inference. If this is true, then the guiding principle of "I will accept my perceptions as true until proven wrong" will tend to guarantee more confirmation than disconfirmation and hence will promote stability.

Perceptions produce confirming evidence. Finally, we should recognize the possibility that the behavior of others can be influenced by our perceptions of them. This sort of pattern has been recognized for some time in the social sciences. The sociologist Robert K. Merton has termed it the "self-fulfilling prophecy."

> The self-fulfilling prophecy is, in the beginning, a false definition of the situation evoking a new behavior which makes the originally false conception come true. The specious validity of the self-fulfilling prophecy perpetuates a reign of error. For the prophet will cite the actual course of events as proof that he was right from the very beginning. . . . Such are the perversities of social logic.*

Although there is considerable anecdotal evidence for the existence of self-fulfilling prophecies, there is surprisingly little research evidence. Rosenthal and Jacobson (1968) were able to show that when teachers were told that certain students would increase their IQ levels during the year, the performance of those students did tend to increase. There are certain methodological problems with this research; for our purposes the findings are merely suggestive evidence since the authors did not attempt to show what teacher-behaviors mediated the changes.

In the absence of empirical data, we can consider a couple of examples of how self-fulfilling prophecies might operate. One sequence might run something like the following: (1) *A* perceives *B* as friendly, (2) *A* behaves toward *B* in a friendly fashion, (3) *B* perceives *A* as being friendly to him, and (4) *B* behaves in a friendly fashion to *A*. That sequence is of course common and the stuff of which friendships are made. Notice that, for whatever reason *A* perceives *B* as friendly, he has initiated a sequence of perceptions and contingent behaviors which seem to build on themselves. A recent study by Feldman and Kleck (1970) provides some data on this issue. They instructed subjects that they would be interacting with a cold (or warm) other. The other was actually a confederate who behaved in a consistent predetermined manner and who did not know whether the subject had been given the warm or cold instructions. The investigators found that the subjects with the warm expectation sat nearer to the confederate than did the subjects with the cold expectation.

For the moment let us consider a less benign and more complete example. *A* and *B* enter into discussion. In the course of the conversation *B* admits that he is a former mental patient. *A* in turn attaches great importance to this characteristic, and it operates as a central trait in his implicit theory of personality. Specifically, *A* believes that mental patients are frequently hostile and quite unpredictable. For *A* a pleasant conversation has been transformed into a potentially

---

*Robert K. Merton, *The Social Theory and Social Structure* (New York: The Free Press, 1957), p. 423.

harmful encounter, and *A* begins to act distant and cold to *B*, who in turn perceives the change in *A*'s behavior and is angered by it. *B* begins to act in a hostile and angry way to *A*, who perceives his anger and becomes frightened. *A* quickly terminates the conversation and leaves, still more convinced than he was before that mental patients (even former ones) are indeed unpredictable and hostile.

The key elements in that sequence of events were the inference processes by *A* and the behavior *A* exhibited contingent on his inference. That behavior in turn elicited behavior from *B* which confirmed *A*'s suspicions about how mental patients behave. Thus the behaviors contingent on certain perceptions forced confirming behavior from the other. The problem of forcing behavior toward confirmation of perception deserves careful research attention.

We have surely not exhausted the possible explanations of why our perceptual systems remain as stable as they do. But we have tried to indicate that one source of perceptual stability lies in the nature of social interactions and the effects of our perceptions on our own and others' behavior.

As an example of the operation of these tendencies, we will discuss the perception of stigmatized others. Unfortunately, this important social problem has received little research attention. Since we lack extensive experimental evidence, we will rely heavily on descriptive accounts of the perception of the stigmatized.

Stigma may be defined as any characteristic which is negatively evaluated by large numbers of people. Physical handicap, mental illness or incapacity, nonwhite skin color, lack of athletic ability, and homosexuality are examples of characteristics which are considered stigmas in at least some circumstances.

Goffman most carefully captures the flavor of what we hope to say:

> By definition, of course, we believe the person with a stigma is not quite human. On this assumption we exercise varieties of discrimination, through which we effectively, if often unthinkingly reduce his life chances. We construct a stigma-theory, an ideology to explain his inferiority and account for the danger he represents. . . . We tend to impute a wide range of imperfections on the basis of the original one, and at the same time to impute some desirable but undesired attributes, often of a supernatural case, such as "sixth sense" or "understanding." Further, we may perceive his defensive response to his situation as a direct expression of his defect, and then see both defect and response as just retribution for something he or his parents or his tribe did, and hence a justification of the way we treat him.*

---

*Erving Goffman, *Stigma: Notes on the Management of Spoiled Identity*, © 1963, pp. 5–6. Quoted by permission of Prentice-Hall, Inc., Englewood Cliffs, N.J.

In our terms, Goffman seems to be saying that stigma operates as a central trait in an implicit theory of personality. We have a stereotype about the stigmatized. If our earlier analyses are correct, there should be a variety of mechanisms for stabilizing that stereotype, some of which Goffman hints at.

In the first place, we argued that many inferences drawn from a stereotype are accurate. If the stereotype suggests that a physically handicapped person would have difficulty doing some things that a nonhandicapped person does with ease, we would probably not be inclined to argue. But inferences do not stop with those easily supported by evidence. As Goffman suggests, "We tend to impute a wide range of imperfections on the basis of the original one. . . . " For example, Chevigny (1946) notes that many people seem to assume the blind are also deaf since they talk louder in the presence of the blind and often talk openly and audibly about them "behind their backs." Other inferred defects, such as unpredictability for the former mental patient, homosexuality for the nonathlete, and intellectual incompetence for the Negro, are far more damaging to the stigmatized person.

Second, we noted that inferences from stereotypes are almost never absolute. Exceptions are allowed. The Helen Kellers and Martin Luther Kings become not only exceptions to the general stereotypic inferences but also, by virtue of their exceptional accomplishments, "credits" to their stigmatized groups. It is interesting that in such cases great emphasis is frequently given to special situational or fortuitous environmental events which allowed the individual to become exceptional. Inadvertently, of course, this emphasis reinforces the stereotype since most members of the stigmatized group presumably do not have the benefit of such luck or special circumstances. Although exceptions to the stereotype are allowed for people with unusual past histories or natural endowments, the more "normal" stigmatized person is bound to be perceived as the rule which creates the exception.

We also mentioned that information flow is biased in such a way that certain kinds of attribution errors are never corrected. There is a great deal of informal and research evidence to indicate that stigmatized people are disliked, and since most "normals" feel uncomfortable interacting with most stigmatized others (Richardson *et al.*, 1961; Kleck, Ono, and Hastorf, 1966), it is reasonable to suppose that they will avoid interactions with the stigmatized. As we have already argued, this hypothesized evasion of interaction reduces the opportunity for the perceiver to correct his inference structure about the stigmatized. Furthermore, as Kleck *et al.* have shown, normals are likely to display a less than usual range of behavior in an interview with a handicapped other. There is actually no direct evidence, but we suspect that normals are unlikely to communicate their real feelings to the stigmatized, and thus there is little real opportunity for the stigmatized to correct a wrong but unstated attribution.

Since interactions between the stigmatized and normals are likely to be perceived as uncomfortable, it is understandable that the stigmatized avoid interaction with normals. Such behavior is particularly common for people with highly visible stigmas. (See MacGregor, 1953, for evidence that this problem is especially acute for people with facial disfigurement.) As Goffman (1963) indicates, the stigmatized are likely to form associations and clubs at least in part to maintain social contact with people with whom they can feel comfortable.

Finally, we note that the stigmatized are frequently forced into roles which merely confirm the perceptions others have of them. As Goffman and others have pointed out, it may become easy for the stigmatized to play the stigma role. Given that many people want to feel sorry for the stigmatized or want to attribute the stigma to real or imagined sins, the stigmatized can expect real benefits from acting in ways which elicit pity; conversely, acting in an independent manner may invite perceptions of ungraciousness. Failure to confess sin may be taken as further evidence of justification for the stigma.

> . . . from the time a man loses his sight, he is fortunate indeed if he is not immediately surrounded by influences which all but insist he accept the viewpoint that the worst catastrophe within the power of the fates to mete out has been meted out to him.*

It is not surprising under these circumstances that many stigmatized people do accept their fate.

Another quotation from the unusually sensitive and informative autobiography of a writer who became blind in middle age illustrates the process even more bluntly. Chevigny describes going to a plush hotel for a haircut and being treated as royalty. Subsequently he discussed the experience with a friend and suggested that he didn't want to be treated differently from a sighted person. Part of their conversation follows.

> "What you don't seem to have taken into your calculations," he said, "is the idea that you will be expected to conform."
>
> "Conform to what?" I asked.
>
> "To a type. You're a blind man now, you'll be expected to act like one."
>
> "I don't want to be a type," I said.

---

*Hector Chevigny, *My Eyes Have a Cold Nose* (New Haven, Conn.; Yale University Press, 1946), p. 153. Copyright © 1946 by Hector Chevigny. Quoted by permission.

"I didn't say that you had to *be* one, I said you'd be expected to act like one. Everybody is expected to act his type if he doesn't want trouble. If you see the president of the bank where you deposit your money carousing in some night club with a lady of doubtful virtue, isn't your first impulse to withdraw your account and put it in the care of some other man who is acting a little more typically? Of course it is. We all instinctively distrust deviations from the norm. An attorney, if he hopes to hold on to his clients, is expected to act and even look like an attorney, a doctor ditto, and so on down the line."

"You're talking about professions," I said. "And stop shoving that ash tray around."

"I don't want you to burn the tablecloth."

"Just leave the ash tray where it is and I won't burn the tablecloth. And I can also light my own cigarettes. Now what about this type business—is the world's first thought that I ought to make a profession of being blind, like selling pencils?"

"In a way. The world's first reaction to you is going to be one of surprise that you make any effort at all not to give up. You've already had a taste of it this morning."

"What do you mean—give up? How can I give up? I have to eat, don't I?"

"You," my friend told me, "are at last in the enviable position of never having to worry any more about eating. *I* can still starve but you will never have to. That's the paradox in your new condition. All you have to do, for all practical purposes, is announce that you can't face what's ahead, that you've given up. Few would doubt your word or even argue about it. In most of our states you'd be granted a pension, and if your family couldn't take care of you there are institutions where you could live out the rest of your days in reasonable comfort and certain security."

For no good reason I could think of at the time, I found this the most disturbing revelation of the day. I hadn't heard it before. I knew about pensions granted the blind when their condition is due to industrial accident, of course, and I heartily approved of the practice. But that the mere fact of blindness should of itself carry the possibility of forever after living off the bounty of society I found a shocking concept. And yet it was also plain that those who do find adjustment an emotional or physical impossibility must be provided for; they cannot be left to die. Here was something else I must think out. I must think it out because in some vague way I felt it a threat to the degree of adjustment I had already achieved. It was disturbing to hear there was an alternative to effort.

"Here's what happened when you walked into that hotel," my friend went on. "They were disturbed, upset to have you come there at all. Not because you were just out of the hospital but because you're blind. That you used to be the kind of client they have there all the time they forgot, if they thought about it at all. They've probably never had a blind man come to that shop before. There is lack of conformity in the idea of your going there and so there was resentment against you."

"Resentment!" I exclaimed. "They couldn't have been kinder."

"Didn't you ever hear about the phenomenon of overcompensation? When an emotional demonstration seems unnatural, look for the thing it is trying to cover. That hotel staff treated you as if you were made of cut glass, and showed you the kind of attention that is reserved for visiting dukes because they had a guilty feeling over their own resentment toward you."

"Sounds complicated," I said.

"It's very simple, really, in fact, it's elementary psychiatry." Speaking of elementary psychiatry, he was no longer moving the ash tray and now I could find it when I needed it. "The world does its thinking in terms of fixed notions. Nothing very profound in that statement. Those fixed notions are things by which journalists like me live. You live by them too—they're at the bottom of every scrap of radio writing you ever did. There are good fixed notions, such as the one that a pretty girl is like a melody; there are ones that don't matter, such as the notion that all fat men are jolly; and there are bad ones, such as the fixed notions about racial or religious minorities. The latter we call prejudices.

"There is now a prejudice against you. That word, as you know, means prejudgment. The same struggle to identify oneself as an individual that lies before a Negro or a Jew or any other member of an identifiable minority group in effect now lies before you too. Whether you like it or not, from now on the world is going to think of you as endowed with a set of characteristics and an attitude that it imagines all blind people have. You can live up to it or you can rebel against it—that is your real choice. And there, incidentally, is the answer to your question as to whether you can or should tell the world how to be kind. It depends on what you want."

"Just what are these characteristics and attitudes with which I'll be endowed from here on out?"

"People will be firmly convinced that you consider yourself a tragedy. They'll be disconcerted and even shocked to discover that you don't."

"Go on."

"Well, that about sums up the attitude they'll endow you with. As for the characteristics, the fixed notion is that blindness renders a man helpless in every way. People will be surprised even to see you get out of a chair."*

---

*Hector Chevigny, *My Eyes Have a Cold Nose* (New Haven, Conn.: Yale University Press, 1946), pp. 71–74. Copyright © 1946 by Hector Chevigny. Quoted by permission.

The point, of course, is that our perceptions of the stigmatized as people to be pitied are often translated into behaviors and verbalized expectations which virtually guarantee that the stigmatized will come to pity themselves. Normals frequently do communicate to the stigmatized that the basis of their relationship must be a pitying-pitied one. To the extent that there is a normative role of the stigmatized, the nonstigmatized have a tendency to perpetuate it.

We should not ignore other forms of perceptions forcing self-confirming behavior. The research of Farina and his colleagues (Farina and Ring, 1965; Farina, Holland, and Ring, 1966; Farina, Sherman, and Allen, 1968; Farina, Allen, and Saul, 1968) has demonstrated that subjects do behave differently, often less charitably, to the stigmatized than to the nonstigmatized. It is probable that the stigmatized will react to such treatment. For example, the ex-mental patient may be provoked by the treatment of others into anger reactions which will in turn be interpreted as manifestations of his malady. We frequently perceive the facially disfigured as hideous, and that perception is all too often communicated to the stigmatized person (MacGregor, 1953). Under these circumstances the disfigured person is likely to approach social situations defensively, and that behavior provides us with further reason to avoid him. Finally, we note that recent Negro militancy and anger at white middle-class racism is often interpreted by whites as further support for the negative stereotype of the Negro.

In the final analysis, there are complex relationships between our perceptions of others and our behavior toward them. We have suggested that perceptions and meaning both guide the behavior of each individual and are created by him in his encounters with others. Whether or not he is accurate in his perceptions may be less critical than whether he reaches a consensual meaning and set of definitions with important others in his life space.

Asch (1952) has best summarized this position:

> The paramount fact about social interaction is that the participants stand on common ground, that they turn toward one another, that their acts interpenetrate and therefore regulate each other.*

This feature of social interaction, indeed of humanness, greatly complicates the scientific analysis of person perception and social behavior, but it makes possible our own understanding of the behavior of others at the common-sense level.

> It is individuals with the particular capacity to turn toward one another who in concrete action validate and consolidate in each a

---

*Solomon Asch, *Social Psychology,* © 1952, p. 161. Quoted by permission of Prentice-Hall, Inc., Englewood Cliffs, N.J.

> *mutually shared field*, one that includes both the surroundings and one another's psychological properties as the objective sphere of action.*

If one thinks about it, he realizes that social psychologists have paid considerable attention to the coordination of behavior (Gergen, 1969) but remarkably little to the coordination of meaning. We now know a great deal about how two persons can come to interact and guide each other's behavior so as to accomplish a task. We do not know nearly enough about how they come to share a common perception of the world. We need to know more about how people get to know one another; such knowledge would entail the matching of one person's perception of another with the other's perception of himself. Precisely defined roles and normative rules, once existing, grease the mechanics of interpersonal behavior in that they provide shared rules for behavior, but by the same token, they may reduce the chances for interpersonal attribution. Roles and norms, perceived as external forces, may lessen the tendency to search out the other's definition of the situation. We know all too little about the variables that lead one group of people to interact and develop shared meanings and another group to interact and not develop coordination of meaning. We hope that increased attention will be paid to the variables that influence the development of shared meaning, for it is a salient part of the fabric of all social life.

**Ibid.*, p. 163

References

Adorno, T. W., Else Frenket-Brunswik, D. Levinson, and R. N. Sanford. *The authoritarian personality.* New York: Harper and Row, 1950.

Allport, G. W. *Personality: a psychological interpretation.* New York: Holt, 1937.

Allport, G. W. *Pattern and growth in personality.* New York: Holt, 1961.

Anderson, N. H. Application of an additive model to impression formation. *Science*, 1962, **138**, 817–818.

Anderson, N. H. Adding versus averaging as a stimulus combination rule in impression formation. *Journal of Experimental Psychology*, 1965, **70**, 394–400.

Anderson, N. H. Component ratings in impression formation. *Psychonomic Science*, 1966, **6**, 279–280.

Anderson, N. H. Likableness ratings of 555 personality trait words. *Journal of Personality and Social Psychology*, 1968(a), **9**, 272–279.

Anderson, N. H. Application of a linear-serial model to a personality-impression task using serial presentation. *Journal of Personality and Social Psychology*, 1968(b), **10**, 354–362.

Anderson, N. H., and S. Hubert. Effects of concomitant verbal recall on order effects in personality impression formation. *Journal of Verbal Learning and Verbal Behavior*, 1963, **2**, 379–391.

Anderson, N. H., and Ann Jacobson. Effect of stimulus inconsistency and discounting instructions in personality impression formation. *Journal of Personality and Social Psychology*, 1965, **2**, 531–539.

Anderson, N. H., and Anita K. Lampel. Effect of context on ratings of personality traits. *Psychonomic Science*, 1965, **3**, 433–434.

Asch, S. E. Forming impressions of personality. *Journal of Abnormal and Social Psychology*, 1946, **41**, 258–290.

Asch, S. E. *Social psychology*. Englewood Cliffs, N.J.: Prentice-Hall, 1952.

Bandler, R. J., Jr., G. R. Madaras, and D. J. Bem. Self-observation as a source of pain perception. *Journal of Personality and Social Psychology*, 1968, **9**, 205–209.

Bavelas, A., A. H. Hastorf, A. E. Gross, and W. R. Kite. Experiments on the alteration of group structure. *Journal of Experimental Social Psychology*, 1965, **1**, 55–70.

Bem, D. J. An experimental analysis of self-persuasion. *Journal of Experimental Social Psychology*, 1965, **1**, 199–218.

Bem, D. J. Self-perception: an alternative interpretation of cognitive dissonance phenomena. *Psychological Review*, 1967, **74**, 183–200.

Bem, D. J. The epistemological status of interpersonal simulations: a reply to Jones, Linder, Kiesler, Zanna and Brehm. *Journal of Experimental Social Psychology*, 1968, **4**, 270–274.

Bender, I. E., and A. H. Hastorf. On measuring generalized empathic ability (social sensitivity). *Journal of Abnormal and Social Psychology*, 1953, **48**, 503–506.

Berkowitz, L. *Aggression: a social psychological analysis*. New York: McGraw-Hill, 1962.

Bruner, J. S., D. Shapiro, and R. Tagiuri. The meaning of traits in isolation and combination. In R. Tagiuri and L. Petrullo (eds.), *Person perception and interpersonal behavior*. Stanford, Calif.: Stanford University Press, 1958.

Bruner, J. S., and R. Tagiuri. Person perception. In G. Lindzey (ed.), *Handbook of social psychology*, Vol. 2. Reading, Mass.: Addison-Wesley, 1954.

Brunswik, E. *Perception and the representative design of psychological experiments*, 2nd ed., rev. and enl. Berkeley: University of California Press, 1956.

Burnstein, E., and P. Worchel. Arbitrariness of frustration and its consequences for aggression in a social situation. *Journal of Personality*, 1962, **30**, 528–541.

Byrne, D. *An introduction to personality*. Englewood Cliffs, N.J.: Prentice-Hall, 1966.

Chevigny, H. *My eyes have a cold nose*. New Haven, Conn.: Yale University Press, 1946.

Cline, V. B. Interpersonal perception. In B. A. Maher (ed.), *Progress in experimental personality research*, Vol. 1. New York: Academic Press, 1964.

Cline, V. B., and J. M. Richards, Jr. Accuracy of interpersonal perception—a general trait? *Journal of Abnormal and Social Psychology*, 1960, **60**, 1–7.

Cohen, A. R. Cognitive tuning as a factor affecting impression formation. *Journal of Personality*, 1961, **29**, 235–245.

Coleman, J. C. Facial expressions of emotion. *Psychological Monographs*, 1949, **63**, No. 1 (Whole No. 296).

Crockett, W. H. Cognitive complexity and impression formation. In B. A.

Maher (ed.), *Progress in experimental personality research*, Vol. 2. New York: Academic Press, 1965.

Cronbach, L. J. Processes affecting scores on "understanding of others" and "assumed similarity." *Psychological Bulletin*, 1955, **52**, 177–193.

Crow, W. J., and K. R. Hammond. The generality of accuracy and response in interpersonal perception. *Journal of Abnormal and Social Psychology*, 1957, **54**, 384–390.

Dailey, C. A. The effects of premature conclusion upon the acquisition of understanding of a person. *Journal of Psychology*, 1952, **33**, 133–152.

D'Andrade, R. G. Trait psychology and componential analysis. *American Anthropologist*, 1965, **67**, 215–228.

Darwin, C. *The expression of the emotions in man and animals*. London: Murray, 1872.

Davison, G. C., and S. Valins. Maintenance of self-attributed and drug-attributed behavior change. *Journal of Personality and Social Psychology*, 1969, **11**, 25–33.

Davitz, J. R. (ed.). *The communication of emotional meaning*. New York: McGraw-Hill, 1964.

deCharms, R. *Personal causation*. New York: Academic Press, 1968.

Dickoff, Hilda. Reactions to evaluations by another person as a function of self evaluation and the interaction context. Unpublished doctoral dissertation, Duke University, 1961.

Dornbusch, S. M., A. H. Hastorf, S. A. Richardson, R. E. Muzzy, and Rebecca S. Vreeland. The perceiver and perceived: their relative influence on categories of interpersonal perception. *Journal of Personality and Social Psychology*, 1965, **1**, 434–440.

Dymond, Rosalind F. A scale for the measurement of emphathic ability. *Journal of Consulting Psychology*, 1949, **13**, 127–133.

Dymond, Rosalind F. Personality and empathy. *Journal of Consulting Psychology*, 1950, **14**, 343–350.

Eisinger, R., and J. Mills. Perception of the sincerity and competence of a communicator as a function of the extremity of his position. *Journal of Experimental Social Psychology*, 1968, **4**, 224–232.

Ekman, P., E. R. Sorenson, and W. V. Friesen. Pan-cultural elements in facial displays of emotion. *Science*, 1969, **164**, 86–88.

Ellsworth, Phoebe C., and J. M. Carlsmith. Effects of eye contact and verbal content on affective response to a dyadic interaction. *Journal of Personality and Social Psychology*, 1968, **10**, 15–20.

Estes, S. G. Judging personality from expressive behavior. *Journal of Abnormal and Social Psychology*, 1938, **33**, 217–236.

Exline, R. V., D. Gray, and D. Schuette. Visual behavior in a dyad as affected by interview content and sex of respondent. *Journal of Personality and Social Psychology*, 1965, **1**, 201–209.

Exline, R. V., and L. C. Winters. Affective relations and mutual glances in dyads. In S. S. Tomkins and C. E. Izard (eds.), *Affect, cognition, and personality.* New York: Springer, 1965.

Farina, A., J. G. Allen, and B. B. Saul. The role of the stigmatized person in affecting social relationships. *Journal of Personality*, 1968, **36**, 169–182.

Farina, A., C. H. Holland, and K. Ring. Role of stigma and set in interpersonal interaction. *Journal of Abnormal Psychology*, 1966, **71**, 421–428.

Farina, A., and K. Ring. The influence of perceived mental illness on interpersonal relations. *Journal of Abnormal and Social Psychology*, 1965, **70**, 47–51.

Farina, A., M. Sherman, and J. G. Allen. Role of physical abnormalities in interpersonal perception and behavior. *Journal of Abnormal Psychology*, 1968, **73**, 590–593.

Feldman, S., and R. E. Kleck. Non-verbal behavior as a function of impression sets. Mimeographed, 1970.

Feleky, Antoinette M. The expression of the emotions. *Psychological Review*, 1914, **21**, 33–41.

Festinger, L. *A theory of cognitive dissonances.* Evanston, Ill.: Row, Peterson, 1957.

Festinger, L., and J. M. Carlsmith. Cognitive consequences of forced compliance. *Journal of Abnormal and Social Psychology*, 1959, **58**, 203–211.

Fiedler, F. E. Interpersonal perception and group effectiveness. In R. Tagiuri and L. Petrullo (eds.), *Person perception and interpersonal behavior.* Stanford, Calif.: Stanford University Press, 1958.

Fiedler, F. E. *A Theory of leadership effectiveness.* New York: McGraw-Hill, 1967.

Fielder, F. E. A contingency model of leadership effectiveness. In L. Berkowitz (ed.), *Advances in experimental social psychology.* New York: Academic Press, 1964.

Fink, K., and H. Cantril. The collegiate stereotype as frame of reference. *Journal of Abnormal and Social Psychology*, 1937, **32**, 352–356.

Frijda, N. H. Recognition of emotion. In L. Berkowitz (ed.), *Advances in experimental social psychology*, Vol. 4. New York: Academic Press, 1969.

Fukuda, Judy. Personal communication, 1969.

Gergen, K. *The psychology of behavior exchange.* Reading, Mass.: Addison-Wesley, 1969.

Goffman, E. On face work: an analysis of ritual elements in social interaction. *Psychiatry*, 1955, **18**, 213–231.

Goffman, E. *Stigma: notes on the management of spoiled identity.* Englewood Cliffs, N.J.: Prentice-Hall, 1963.

Gollin, E. S. Forming impressions of personality. *Journal of Personality*, 1954, **23**, 65–76.

Gollin, E. S., and S. Rosenberg. Concept formation and impressions of personality. *Journal of Abnormal and Social Psychology*, 1956, **52**, 39–42.

Gouldner, A. W. The norm of reciprocity: a preliminary statement. *American Sociological Review*, 1960, **25**, 161–178.

Green, B. F. Attitude measurement. In G. Lindzey (ed.), *Handbook of social psychology*, Vol. 1. Reading, Mass.: Addison-Wesley, 1954.

Gross, A. Evaluation of the target person in a social influence situation. Unpublished doctoral dissertation, Stanford University, 1966.

Haire, M., and Willa F. Grunes. Perceptual defenses: processes protecting an organized perception of another personality. *Human Relations*, 1950, **3**, 403–412.

Hakel, M. Significance of implicit personality theories for personality research and theory. *Proceedings of the American Psychological Association*, 1969.

Harvey, O. J., D. E. Hunt, and H. M. Schroder. *Conceptual systems and personality organization*. New York: Wiley, 1961.

Hastorf, A. H., and I. E. Bender. A caution respecting the measurement of emphathic ability. *Journal of Abnormal and Social Psychology*, 1952, **47**, 574–576.

Hastorf, A. H., and H. Cantril. They saw a game: a case study. *Journal of Abnormal and Social Psychology*, 1954, **49**, 129–134.

Hastorf, A. H., W. R. Kite, A. E. Gross, and Lyn J. Wolfe. The perception and evaluation of behavior change. *Sociometry*, 1965, **48**, 400–410.

Hastorf, A. H., S. A. Richardson, and S. M. Dornbusch. The problem of relevance in the study of person perception. In R. Tagiuri and L. Petrullo (eds.), *Person perception and interpersonal behavior*. Stanford, Calif.: Stanford University Press, 1958.

Heider, F. Social perception and phenomenal causality. *Psychological Review*, 1944, **51**, 358–374.

Heider, F. *The psychology of interpersonal relations*. New York: Wiley, 1958.

Heider, F., and Marianne Simmel. An experimental study of apparent behavior. *American Journal of Psychology*, 1944, **57**, 243–259.

Jackson, D. N. The measurement of perceived personality trait relationships. In D. Willner (ed.), *Decisions, values, and groups*, Vol. 2. New York: Pergamon Press, 1962.

Jackson, D. N., S. Messick, and C. M. Solley. A multidimensional scaling approach to the perception of personality. *Journal of Psychology*, 1957, **44**, 311–318.

James, W. *The principles of psychology*. New York: Holt, 1890.

Johnson, T. J., R. Feigenbaum, and M. Weibey. Some determinants and consequences of the teacher's perception of causality. *Journal of Educational Psychology*, 1964, **55**, 237–246.

Jones, E. E. Authoritarianism as a determinant of first-impression formation. *Journal of Personality*, 1954, **23**, 107–127.

Jones, E. E. *Ingratiation: a social psychological analysis*. New York: Appleton-Century-Crofts, 1964.

Jones, E. E., and K. E. Davis. From acts to dispositions: the attribution process in person perception. In L. Berkowitz (ed.), *Advances in experimental social psychology*, Vol. 2. New York: Academic Press, 1965.

Jones, E. E., K. E. Davis, and K. J. Gergen. Role playing variations and their informational value for person perception. *Journal of Abnormal and Social Psychology*, 1961, **63**, 302–310.

Jones, E. E. and R. deCharms. Changes in social perception as a function of the personal relevance of behavior. *Sociometry*, 1957, **20**, 75–85.

Jones, E. E., and V. A. Harris. The attribution of attitudes. *Journal of Experimental Social Psychology*, 1967, **3**, 1–24.

Jones, E. E., L. Rock, K. G. Shaver, G. R. Goethals, and L. M. Ward. Pattern performance and ability attribution: an unexpected primacy effect. *Journal of Personality and Social Psychology*, 1968, **10**, 317–341.

Jones, R. A., D. E. Linder, C. A. Kiesler, M. Zanna, and J. W. Brehm. Internal states or external stimuli: observers' attitude judgments and the dissonance theory–self persuasion controversy. *Journal of Experimental Social Psychology*, 1968, **4**, 247–269.

Karlins, M., T. L. Coffman, and G. Walters. On the fading of social stereotypes: studies in three generations of college students. *Journal of Personality and Social Psychology*, 1969, **13**, 1–16.

Katz, D., and K. W. Braley. Racial stereotypes of one hundred college students. *Journal of Abnormal and Social Psychology*, 1933, **28**, 280–290.

Kelley, H. H. The warm-cold variable in first impressions of persons. *Journal of Personality*, 1950, **18**, 431–439.

Kelley, H. H. Attribution theory in social psychology. *Nebraska Symposium on Motivation*, 1967, **15**, 192–238.

Kelly, G. A. *The psychology of personal constructs*. New York: Norton, 1955.

Kenny, D. T., and R. Ginsberg. The specificity of intolerance of ambiguity measures. *Journal of Abnormal and Social Psychology*, 1958, **56**, 300–304.

Kiesler, C. A., and Sara B. Kiesler. *Conformity*. Reading, Mass.: Addison-Wesley, 1969.

Kiesler, C. A., R. E. Nisbett, and M. P. Zanna. On inferring one's beliefs from one's behavior. *Journal of Personality and Social Psychology*, 1969, **11**, 321–327.

Kite, W. R. Attributions of causality as a function of the use of reward and punishment. Unpublished doctoral dissertation, Stanford University, 1964.

Kleck, R., H. Ono, and A. H. Hastorf. The effects of physical deviance upon face-to-face interaction. *Human Relations*, 1966, **19**, 425–436.

Klineberg, O. Emotional expression in Chinese literature. *Journal of Abnormal and Social Psychology*, 1938, **33**, 517–520.

Koltuv, Barbara. Some characteristics of intrajudge trait intercorrelations. *Psychological Monographs*, 1962, **76** (33, Whole No. 552).

Landis, C. Studies of emotional reactions: II. General behavior and facial expression. *Journal of Comparative Psychology*, 1924, **4**, 447–509.

Landy, D., and E. Aronson. Liking for an evaluator as a function of his discernment. *Journal of Personality and Social Psychology*, 1968, **9**, 133–141.

Lanzetta, J. T., and T. E. Hannah. Reinforcing behavior of "naive" trainers. *Journal of Personality and Social Psychology*, 1969, **11**, 245–252.

Lay, C. H., and D. N. Jackson. Analysis of the generality of trait-inferential relationships. *Journal of Personality and Social Psychology*, 1969, **12**, 12–21.

Leeper, R. The role of motivation in learning: a study of the phenomenon of differential motivation control of the utilization of habits. *Journal of Genetic Psychology*, 1935, **46**, 3–40.

Leventhal, H. The effects of set and discrepancy on impression change. *Journal of Personality*, 1962, **30**, 1–15.

Leventhal, H., and D. L. Singer. Cognitive complexity, impression formation and impression change. *Journal of Personality*, 1964, **32**, 210–226.

Luchins, A. S. Forming impressions of personality: a critique. *Journal of Abnormal and Social Psychology*, 1948, **43**, 318–325.

Luchins, A. S. Primacy-recency in impression formation. In C. Hovland (ed.), *The order of presentation in persuasion*. New Haven, Conn.: Yale University Press, 1957(a).

Luchins, A. S. Experimental attempts to minimize the impact of first impressions. In C. Hovland (ed.), *The order of presentation in persuasion*. New Haven, Conn.: Yale University Press, 1957(b).

Luchins, A. S. Definiteness of impression and primacy-recency in communications. *Journal of Social Psychology*, 1958, **48**, 275–290.

MacGregor, Frances C. *Facial deformities and plastic surgery*. Springfield, Ill.: Thomas, 1953.

Mayo, Clara W., and W. H. Crockett. Cognitive complexity and primacy-recency effects in impression formation. *Journal of Abnormal and Social Psychology*, 1964, **68**, 335–388.

Mead, G. H. *Mind, self and society*. Chicago: University of Chicago Press, 1934.

Merton, R. K. *Social theory and social structure*. New York: Free Press, 1957.

Messick, S., and N. Kogan. Personality consistencies in judgment: dimension of role constructs. *Multivariate Behavioral Research*, 1966, **1**, 165–175.

Michotte, A. *Perception of causality*. New York: Basic Books, 1963.

Mills, J., and J. M. Jellison. Effect of opinion change of how desirable the communication is to the audience the communicator addressed. *Journal of Personality and Social Psychology*, 1967, **6**, 98–101.

Mischel, W. *Personality and assessment*. New York: Wiley, 1968.

Mulaik, S. A. Are personality factors raters' conceptual factors? *Journal of Consulting Psychology*, 1964, **28**, 506–511.

Newcomb, T. M. An experiment designed to test the validity of a rating technique. *Journal of Educational Psychology*, 1931, **22**, 279–289.

Newcomb, T. M. Autistic hostility and social reality. *Human Relations*, 1947, **1**, 69–87.

Newcomb, T. M. *The acquaintance process*. New York: Holt, Rinehart and Winston, 1961.

Nisbett, R. E., and S. Schachter. Cognitive manipulation of pain. *Journal of Experimental Psychology*, 1966, **2**, 227–236.

Norman, W. T. Toward an adequate taxonomy of personality attributes: replicated factor structure in peer nomination personality ratings. *Journal of Abnormal and Social Psychology*, 1963, **66**, 574–583.

Osgood, C. E. Dimensionality of the semantic space for communication via facial expressions. *Scandinavian Journal of Psychology*, 1966, **7**, 1–30.

Osgood, C., G. J. Suci, and P. H. Tannenbaum. *The measurement of meaning*. Urbana, Ill.: University of Illinois Press, 1957.

Osgood, C., and P. H. Tannenbaum. The principle of congruity and the prediction of attitude change. *Psychological Review*, 1955, **62**, 42–55.

Passini, F. T., and W. T. Norman. A universal conception of personality structure? *Journal of Personality and Social Psychology*, 1966, **4**, 44–49.

Pastore, N. The role of arbitrariness in the frustration-aggression hypothesis. *Journal of Abnormal and Social Psychology*, 1952, **47**, 728–731.

Pepitone, A., and R. Hayden. Some evidence for conflict resolution in impression formation. *Journal of Abnormal and Social Psychology*, 1955, **51**, 302–307.

Pepitone, A., and J. Sherberg. Cognitive factors in interpersonal attraction. *Journal of Personality*, 1957, **25**, 757–766.

Piaget, J. *The child's conception of physical causality*. New York: Harcourt, Brace, 1930.

Polefka, Judith T. The perception and evaluation of responses to social influence. Unpublished doctoral dissertation, Stanford University, 1965.

Richardson, S. A., N. Goodman, A. H. Hastorf, and S. M. Dornbusch. Cultural uniformity in reaction to physical disabilities. *American Sociological Review*, 1961, **26**, 241–247.

Rosenberg, S., C. Nelson, and P. S. Vivekananthan. A multidimensional approach to the structure of personality impressions. *Journal of Personality and Social Psychology*, 1968, **9**, 283–294.

Rosenkrantz, P. S., and W. Crockett. Some factors influencing the assimilation of disparate information in impression formation. *Journal of Personality and Social Psychology*, 1965, **2**, 397–402.

Rosenthal, R., and Lenore Jacobson. *Pygmalion in the classroom*. New York: Holt, Rinehart and Winston, 1968.

Rothbart, M. Effects of motivation, equity and compliance on the use of reward and punishment. *Journal of Personality and Social Psychology*, 1968, **9**, 353–362.

Schachter, S. The interaction of cognitive and physiological determinants of emotional state. In L. Berkowitz (ed.), *Advances in experimental social psychology*, Vol. 1. New York: Academic Press, 1964.

Schachter, S., and J. E. Singer. Cognitive, social, and physiological determinants of emotional state. *Psychological Review*, 1962, **69**, 379–399.

Schachter, S., and L. Wheeler. Epinephrine, chlorpromazine, and amusement. *Journal of Abnormal and Social Psychology*, 1962, **65**, 121–128.

Schafer, R., and G. Murphy. The role of autism in a visual figure-ground relationship. *Journal of Experimental Psychology*, 1943, **32**, 335–343.

Schlosberg, H. The description of facial expressions in terms of two dimensions. *Journal of Experimental Psychology*, 1952, **44**, 229–237.

Schlosberg, H. Three dimensions of emotion. *Psychological Review*, 1954, **61**, 81–88.

Schneider, D. J. The perception of approval as a function of recipient expectation and evaluator discrimination. Unpublished mimeographed paper, 1965.

Schneider, D. J. Tactical self-presentation after success and failure. *Journal of Personality and Social Psychology*, 1969, **13**, 262–268.

Schmitt, D. R. The invocation of moral obligation. *Sociometry*, 1964, **27**, 299–310.

Schroder, H. M., M. J. Driver, and S. Streufert. *Human information processing*. New York: Holt, Rinehart and Winston, 1967.

Scott, W. A. Cognitive complexity and cognitive balance. *Sociometry*, 1963, **26**, 66–74.

Shapiro, D., and R. Tagiuri. Sex differences in inferring personality traits. *Journal of Psychology*, 1959, **47**, 127–136.

Shaw, M. E. Some cultural differences in sanctioning behavior. *Psychonomic Science*, 1967, **8**, 45–46.

Shaw, M. E., and J. L. Sulzer. An empirical test of Heider's levels in attribution of responsibility. *Journal of Abnormal and Social Psychology*, 1964, **69**, 39–46.

Steiner, I. D. Ethnocentrism and tolerance of trait "inconsistency." *Journal of Abnormal and Social Psychology*, 1954, **49**, 349–354.

Steiner, I. D., and W. L. Field. Role assignment and interpersonal influence. *Journal of Abnormal and Social Psychology*, 1960, **61**, 239–245.

Steiner, I. D., and H. H. Johnson. Authoritarianism and "tolerance of trait inconsistency." *Journal of Abnormal and Social Psychology*, 1963, **67**, 388–391.

Stewart, R. Effect of continuous responding on the order effect in personality impression formation. *Journal of Personality and Social Psychology*, 1965, **1**, 161–165.

Strachey, L. *Eminent Victorians*. New York: Modern Library, 1933 (also available in paperback, Capricorn, 1963).

Streufert, S., and Susan C. Streufert. Effects of conceptual structure, failure, and success on attribution of causality and interpersonal attitudes. *Journal of Personality and Social Psychology*, 1969, **11**, 138–147.

Strickland, L. H. Surveillance and trust. *Journal of Personality*, 1958, **26**, 200–215.

Sulzer, J. L., and R. K. Burglass. Responsibility attribution, empathy and punitiveness. *Journal of Personality*, 1968, **36**, 272–282.

Taft, R. The ability to judge people. *Psychological Bulletin*, 1955, **52**, 1–23.

Tagiuri, R. Person perception. In G. Lindzey and E. Aronson (eds.), *The handbook of social psychology*, Vol. 3. Reading, Mass.: Addison-Wesley, 1969.

Tagiuri, R., R. R. Blake, and J. S. Bruner. Some determinants of the perception of positive and negative feelings in others. *Journal of Abnormal and Social Psychology*, 1953, **48**, 585–592.

Thibaut, J. W., and H. H. Kelley. *The social psychology of groups*. New York: Wiley, 1959.

Thibaut, J. W., and H. W. Riecken. Some determinants and consequences of the perception of social causality. *Journal of Personality*, 1955, **24**, 113–133.

Thorndike, E. L. A constant error in psychological ratings. *Journal of Applied Psychology*, 1920, **4**, 25–29.

Todd, F. J., and L. Rappoport. A cognitive structure approach to person perception: a comparison of two models. *Journal of Abnormal and Social Psychology*, 1964, **68**, 469–478.

Triandis, H. C., and M. Fishbein. Cognitive interaction in person perception. *Journal of Abnormal and Social Psychology*, 1963, **67**, 446–453.

Valins, S. Cognitive effects of false heart-rate feedback. *Journal of Personality and Social Psychology*, 1966, **4**, 400–408.

Valins, S., and A. A. Ray. Effects of cognitive desensitization of avoidance behavior. *Journal of Personality and Social Psychology*, 1967, **7**, 345–350.

Vernon, P. E. Some characteristics of the good judge of personality. *Journal of Social Psychology*, 1933, **4**, 42–58.

Walster, Elaine. The assignment of responsibility for an accident. *Journal of Personality and Social Psychology*, 1966, **5**, 508–516.

Walters, H. A., and D. N. Jackson. Group and individual regularities in trait inference: a multidimensional scaling analysis. *Multivariate Behavioral Research*, 1966, **1**, 145–163.

Warr, P. B., and C. Knapper. *The perception of people and events*. New York: Wiley, 1968.

Warr, P. B., and A. Sims. A study of cojudgment processes. *Journal of Personality*, 1965, **33**, 598–604.

Wiggins, Nancy, P. Hoffman, and T. Taber. Types of judges and cue utilization in judgments of intelligence. *Journal of Personality and Social Psychology*, 1969, **12**, 52–59.

Wishner, J. Reanalysis of "Impressions of personality." *Psychological Review*, 1960, **67**, 96–112.

Witkin, H. A., R. B. Dyk, Hanna F. Faterson, D. R. Goodenough, and S. A. Karp. *Psychological differentiation: studies of development*. New York: Wiley, 1962.

Woodworth, R. S. *Experimental psychology*. New York: Holt, 1938.

Wyer, R. S., and M. Dermer. Effect of context and instructional set upon evaluations of personality-trait adjectives. *Journal of Personality and Social Psychology*, 1968, **9**, 7–14.

Wyer, R. S., and S. F. Watson. Context effects in impression formation. *Journal of Personality and Social Psychology*, 1969, **12**, 22–33.

Zajonc, R. The process of cognitive tuning in communication. *Journal of Abnormal and Social Psychology*, 1960, **61**, 159–167.

Zimbardo, P. G., and E. B. Ebbesen. *Influencing attitudes and changing behavior*. Reading, Mass.: Addison-Wesley, 1969.